The Insider's Guide to
COMPLETE ASSET PROTECTION

■

by Brett K. Kates, Esq.

Enterprise Publishing, Inc.

725 North Market Street, Wilmington, DE 19801 (302) 654-0110

Printed in the United States of America

Contents

i

How to Use Your Insiders' Guide to Complete Asset Protection

1

It is virtually impossible to pick up a newspaper today and not see a striking article about a multi-million dollar lawsuit that has been brought against a business person or a professional. In virtually every one of those cases the defendants' personal assets—their savings, their securities, their personal possessions, even their homes—are put at risk because of unanticipated lawsuits.

The targets of those lawsuits are not just Fortune 500 corporations. They include the doctor who is sued for an evaluation he or she may have made two years ago, the businessman whose corporation inadvertently caused a pollution problem, and the homeowner whose guest slipped and fell and now sues for ten million dollars.

But, you may wonder, doesn't insurance cover these risks? Yes, to some extent it may. In many cases, it simply does not. Consider the situation of the homeowner who carries homeowner's insurance that provides one million dollars of coverage for accidental injuries. Does that policy provide enough protection if a guest slips and falls and now sues for ten million dollars? How much insurance is enough in today's litigation-prone society? What you must keep in mind is that today's lawyers increasingly urge

their clients to seek greater and greater recoveries. Adding to that is the media hype given to outlandish awards. Is it any wonder that "injured" parties assume that their claim is invaluable, and that in many cases "sensible" insurance coverage simply is not enough?

Nor are the threats to your personal assets limited to those from allegedly injured persons. The Internal Revenue Service may suddenly audit your tax returns and challenge deductions you took on the advice of professional advisors. The Service's claims that you have underpaid your taxes may call for you to pay far more than you have available. Or, a good marriage may turn to ashes, and a friendly divorce may become completely antagonistic as each spouse seeks the lion's share of the family assets. Or, a catastrophic illness can threaten to wipe out a lifetime of savings.

You may also wonder whether the need to protect personal assets is limited to only those who are truly wealthy. Far from it, this need exists for people in all income brackets, except perhaps for those at the very lowest end of the earnings ladder. If you have (1) a home, (2) a bank account, (3) investments in small blocks of corporate securities, (4) valuable family heirlooms; or (5) a special collection of items that you acquired as a hobbyist, your assets are at risk in today's litigious society.

More so than ever before, the bitter facts of life require people who have struggled to create financial security to take extra measures to protect their hard-earned wealth—their homes, their savings, their investments, even their retirement plans.

That is just what this book is about: how you can protect your assets from outside attack, and how you can do it within the parameters of the law. It is important for you to realize that just as legislators and lawyers have come up with a myriad of ways in which you can fall victim to a ruinous financial claim, they have also come up with an almost equal number of ways in which you can protect your assets from those claims.

Lawyers term a person "judgment proof" when he or she has no assets that can be reached by creditors or other claimants. That does not have to mean that the person in question is penniless; rather, it can mean that the person's assets are beyond the reach of a plaintiff or the courts, and that for the purposes of a lawsuit the person must be viewed as being penniless.

Each chapter in this book will describe a legal, practical and uncomplicated approach you can adopt to shield your assets from attack. Not every approach will work for every person. Instead, you will be able to pick and choose among the options so that you can come up with the combination that will work best for you. In order to ensure that you come up with the right blend of tools, we will explain not just the positive aspects of each approach but also the negative features so that you can make an intelligent, informed decision.

In reaching your decision as to the right approach for your needs, however, you must first ask yourself several questions. Each of these questions goes to the issue of what your most pressing needs really are. If you are actively engaged in a business or a profession, you may fear attacks from creditors or third persons who claim to have been injured by you in your business or professional

capacity. You may, on the other hand, be more concerned with income or estate taxes. Or, you may have a reason to be more concerned with the possibility of a catastrophic illness. By identifying your specific needs, you will be able to evaluate more fully the advisability of using the various approaches that will be set out in this book. The questions you should ask yourself are:

- Am I engaged in a business or profession? If so, you will want to consider the approaches in this book that protect your assets from attack by (1) creditors and (2) other individuals. Those other individuals may be people who suffer either a physical or financial injury. The physical injury may arise because of your alleged malpractice (if you are a professional such as a doctor, dentist, or therapist), or because of alleged negligence in the way your business or home is operated or maintained, e.g., the person who slips and falls because of a crack in the sidewalk. A financial injury can arise because you and/or your business fails to pay its bills.

- Do your most pressing needs involve the income taxes you are forced to pay? If so, several of the approaches described in this book are especially useful for you. By the same token, several will work against you. We'll take care to point out which approaches have special income tax significance.

- Are you particularly concerned with the drain estate taxes may make when the time comes for those for whom you've worked to provide a good life to inherit your hard-earned assets? Again, some of the approaches we'll describe are designed to protect your assets from estate taxes; some will not offer any protection. We'll note which are which as we discuss each approach.

- Do you have a reason to be concerned with the possibility of a catastrophic illness? If you are over the age of fifty, and you are realistic, then you should have some concern about the drain on your assets that a catastrophic illness will cause. As we'll note in Chapter 7, seven out of every ten people will be forced to come to grips with the need to provide long-term care in our lifetime. There are special approaches you can adopt to ensure that your assets provide you with income while ensuring that the principal generating that income does not fall prey to the claims of health-care providers.

Finally, there is one caution that we must state clearly, strongly and without reservation. Complete asset protection is not a one-person task. A sound program has tax and liability aspects that require professional expertise. Many of the approaches described in this book are based on state legislation; but not all states have the same laws. You should ask your lawyer to review any program that you seek to adopt. Similarly, virtually any transaction involving your assets may have income and estate tax consequences. It would be foolhardy on your part to adopt a program that has tax implications without consulting a professional tax advisor.

What you can expect when you work with this book is that you will have given yourself the ability to map out a powerful asset protection stronghold capable of withstanding even the most brutal attack. The actual construction of that stronghold is something that you will want to do in conjunction with your professional advisors.

The Concept of Asset Protection

2

We live in a most unsettled time. Many people who once had secure jobs now find themselves out of work. Within a short time the newly unemployed use up their savings just to pay for the bare necessities. Not only are their savings wiped out, but shortly they find their other assets subjected to the claims of their creditors.

Equally dangerous to those who have struggled to amass a personal fortune is the fact that we now live in a society enthralled with the idea of making a fortune through litigation. The least of alleged wrongs can lead to a lawsuit in which hundreds of thousands, if not millions, of dollars are sought. I've taught a course for financial planners on risk management and insurance. The course was successful because its primary focus was risk recognition.

Asset protection is based on the recognition of risk and the structuring of your holdings in a manner that will reduce your exposure to risk. The key to risk avoidance, however, is to recognize that attacks on your assets can come from virtually any direction. The list of possible sources of attack includes:

1. Automobile accidents

2. Property accidents, e.g., a business or personal guest slips and falls down a flight of steps

3. Tax liabilities

4. Debts of your business

5. Contract difficulties

6. Child support

7. Alimony

8. Forfeiture of financing notes

9. Malpractice

10. Business breakups

11. The cost of paying the estate of a partner

This is a partial list. It is limited by the imagination of your creditor's attorney. This Guide has been designed to aid you in structuring your holdings so that you can minimize the chance your creditors will take them from you.

To my way of thinking, one of life's tragedies occurs when an individual or family loses their assets. That tragedy is compounded by the fact that we can protect our assets if we are willing to invest some time and thought in "preventative medicine". The best approach is to plan and put your plan into action before a claim arises. As you will protect our assets if we are willing to invest some time and thought in "preventative medicine". The best approach is to plan and put your plan into action before a claim arises. As you will see when we discuss the issue of fraudulent transfer, if you wait until your creditors attack, you may have waited too long to mount an effective counterattack.

Asset Protection Rules and Strategies

1. Plan Ahead.

Many strategies only limit the damage once a claim against assets is made. Planning before the claim is made will provide you with more options and a greater chance of surviving an attack by a creditor. If you try a transfer of property after a judgment, your efforts will prove fruitless. So, for example, before you undertake any venture, particularly a business venture, you should try to select a business form that insulates you from liability (see Chapter 8).

2. Review your plan regularly.

The law is a living thing and changes constantly. Tax laws, for example, are amended virtually every year. Your asset protection program is no less a living thing. As the laws and circumstances change, so too should your plan be adapted to meet changing laws and circumstances. You will be doing yourself a disservice if you do not review and update your plan at least once a year. (If you inherit property or go into a new business venture, or you are sued, review your plan immediately.)

3. Include your whole family.

Just as none of us lives our lives in a vacuum, you should not review your plan in a vacuum. Review it with those family members who have an active interest in your assets and who may have to react to potential problems with speed and decisiveness. Asset protection is not for the individual. It is based on maintaining the maximum asset value within the entire family unit. As will be discussed, communication is the key. You will see that sometimes it makes sense to place assets in certain family members' hands—clear communications will limit any misunderstanding or resentment as to the use of the assets and for whose benefits the assets will be held.

4. Strategize by Objective.

Many management programs require businesses to determine their strategies by what is known as management by objectives. You must do the same. Some asset protection approaches conflict directly with your business goals or tax or estate plans that you may already have in place. In some instances, a particular asset protection tool may hinder your ability to do business. Decide what is important to you and develop your strategy with that goal in mind.

5. Take stock of your property.

No plan can be created in a vacuum. Guessing can be as damaging as having no plan at all. As with any estate plan, you must inventory the following assets:

1. Bank accounts
2. Pension and retirement plans
3. Insurance policies
4. Stocks and bonds
5. Real estate holdings
6. Inheritances
7. Antiques, art and other collectibles and collections
8. Other personal property (assets other than real estate)
9. Loans you may have made to others
10. Business holdings
11. Partnership interests

By the same token, you must inventory your liabilities, including:

1. Mortgages on real estate you own
2. Installment loans

3. Credit card and revolving charge account debt

4. Notes you may have guaranteed or for which you are a co-signor

5. Current lawsuits that may have been brought against you

6. Alimony and/or child support agreements

6. *Be prepared to compromise.*

The most effective asset protection program calls for you to own no assets. The least effective protection program permits you to own everything in your name. Somewhere between those two extremes is the strategy most appropriate for you. The greater the amount of control you relinquish, the greater the protection your property acquires. Only you can measure how much control you can comfortably sacrifice. But, if you want to create an effective asset protection program, you must give up some amount of control.

7. *Build a team.*

Asset protection is a team approach. Not only will your family be involved, but your attorney will be needed to help you structure your ownership correctly. We provide a trust agreement in this book; however, it is still advisable to have an attorney versed in asset protection review your strategy. Although most states do not recognize specialties for lawyers, search for one with experience. A little money invested now can pay tremendous dividends. As one advertisement used to say, "Pay me now, or pay me later." You must make the same decision if you want to protect your family wealth.

8. *Be flexible, be smart.*

Asset protection uses the law to your advantage, not for your creditor's purposes. No plan is cast in concrete. Do not be afraid to use as many of the asset protection tools as are needed for your purposes, and do not be afraid to change your program if changes in the law weaken a tool in your arsenal.

Fraudulent Transfers

Often a debtor will seek to shield assets from a creditor's collection efforts by either hiding or shifting the assets to an "unrelated" outside or third party. Generally the shift to an outside party is conditioned on the debtor's being able to reclaim the property at a later time—that is, when the heat is off. Typically, the recipient of the property usually pays less than the property's fair market value, where fair market value is understood to mean the price at which a willing buyer would buy and a willing seller would sell when neither individual is required to buy or sell. The concept of "fair market value" is vital to the determination of whether a fraudulent transfer has occurred.

There are occasions where a debtor transfers property for less than fair market value without any intent to defraud creditors. Typically this can happen in two situations. First, a gift of property to a relative for less than adequate consideration usually is not made with the intent to defraud creditors or with the preconceived idea that the debtor will reacquire the property at a later date. Second, the debtor's financial situation may be such that he or she is willing to sell property at a bargain basement price in order to raise cash quickly. If such a sale is made to offset outstanding debts and the proceeds of the sale are used for that purpose, a creditor will be hard pressed to demonstrate that the sale was a fraudulent transfer.

Many states have adopted fraudulent conveyance statutes to protect the legitimate rights and claims of creditors against unscrupulous debtors who would shift their assets for the primary purpose of defeating a creditor's ability to collect the debt. However, the claim of a fraudulent conveyance or transfer is far down the line from a creditor's initial claim for a debt owed to it. First the creditor must pursue all appropriate legal avenues, including reducing the debt to a judgment. The creditor now becomes a judgment creditor. Only after a judgment has been entered will the creditor uncover that assets sufficient to satisfy the debt have been shifted to make the debt unrecoverable.

The judgment creditor initially has the burden of demonstrating that the transfer by the debtor rendered the debtor judgment proof. Thereafter, the burden shifts to the debtor to demonstrate that any shifting of assets was not a fraudulent transfer. If the debtor is unable to overcome the presumption that the transfer was fraudulent, the judgment creditor may (1) proceed to execute against the transferred property regardless of whose hands the property is in, or (2) by Court order, force the cancellation of the original transfer. In essence, the recipient of property in a fraudulent conveyance is exposed to what is known as transferee liability.

In addition, fraudulent conveyance laws allow creditors to attempt to attach property that is in jeopardy of being fraudulently transferred. This requires a court to exercise its equitable powers to (1) prohibit a transfer, (2) appoint a receiver to hold the property during the pending litigation, or (3) issue a restraining order. All of these remedies are extraordinary and generally arise only in emergency situations. Courts are generally reluctant to grant such sweeping protections to creditors, since it grants a creditor the status of a "judgment creditor" before a trial on the merits of the creditor's claim.

The theory under which the fraudulent conveyance laws grant the courts such sweeping power is that creditors may be irreparably harmed if the property is not conserved or protected to ensure that it remains available to satisfy a judgment.

Under the law, a fraudulent conveyance will be presumed where an "insolvent" debtor gifts his property to his children. By the very nature of the fact that the transfer is a "gift", it is clear that the creditor received no consideration. In other words, the debtor transferred for less than

fair market value property that is equitably owned by his creditors. The law considers the creditors the owners of the debtor's property when the debtor is insolvent—even though the debtor still legally owns the property. In this situation the law does not require the debtor to have a bad intent. The facts that the property was transferred, even with the honest intention to make a gift, and the transfer was for less than fair market value constitute a fraudulent transfer entitling the creditors to obtain "their" property.

Tip

> *Fair value is determined by the situation. "Retail price" is not necessarily the market price. Fair value at a distress or bankruptcy sale is usually far less than the fair value that could be expected from an arm's-length sale.*

Fair market value is an imprecise term. It has been interpreted by the courts generally to mean what a willing buyer would pay and a willing seller accept when neither party is under the obligation to buy or sell. However, the courts have also recognized that this standard does not define a number, but only generates a reasonable range for value. The issue arises when property has a readily determinable value, so that receiving less than the benchmark price raises the specter of a fraudulent conveyance.

The prime example of this situation would be the sale of a bond that is publicly traded. Such a security has an easily determined trading price at any given time. Should a debtor sell his bond in a private transaction for less than the market price, it is likely that a fraudulent transfer will be found.

Conversely, some property does not have an easily determined fair market value. Antiques and collectibles are prime examples of such property. The price an item would bring at sale is tied to extrinsic issues such as demand, quality, quantity and the general economy. Consider the current real estate market and you will readily see that what may have been a distress price only last year may be considered a very good price in today's market.

Accordingly, fair value and consideration are extremely fact and situation sensitive. There are no strict guidelines; to the contrary, reasonable differences can be expected to occur. Your individual situation must be guided by a reasonable man standard, giving particular attention to recognizing that purchasers may be aware of your financial need. A "motivated" seller can be expected to receive less than a seller not under the obligation to sell.

At the outset of this section we raised the issue of transferee liability. Does that mean that all recipients of property from insolvent debtors are subject to losing what they purchased? No. The Uniform Fraudulent Conveyance Act protects buyers who act in good faith. The good faith buyer takes his title clear of any claims of creditors of the original debtor.

What makes someone a good faith purchaser? The UFCA has developed three standards, all of which must be met by the purchaser:

1. The buyer must have bought the property in "good faith", i.e., the transaction must be a true purchase. As previously discussed, the buyer must not have an arrangement to return the property to the debtor when the "heat is off."

2. The buyer must be unaware of the fact that the debtor entered into the transfer in order to defraud creditors. This standard is tied directly to the issue of good faith. If a buyer knows that the sale constitutes a fraud on creditors of the seller, then the buyer cannot be a good faith purchaser.

3. Fair value must be paid for the property. Should the buyer be too good a negotiator, he may lose the property to the creditors of the seller. The courts, generally, will recognize a distress price; but at certain levels the courts will cease to recognize the sale as bona fide.

If you are a good faith purchaser who has cut too good a deal, you will not lose all of your funds. You are entitled to be reimbursed for the full amount of the price you paid or you will be granted lien against the property until you are made whole. The benefit of your good negotiations is lost, but not your money.

Checklist of Concerns

1. Intent is important in determining a fraudulent transfer. As noted earlier, prior planning will help avoid a claim of fraud. Plan your transfer early.

2. If possible, transfer property to non-family transferees. Transfers to trusted advisers and associates should be your goal since your aim is asset protection, not asset giveaways.

3. The best evidence is the paper. If you have loans or transactions with friends, support them with the right documents. In the chapter on corporations you will learn the importance of maintaining corporate formalities. This should follow through on all of your asset dealings. Creditors will be hard pressed to overturn a properly documented exchange.

4. Show non-protection reasons for transfers. Gifts should demonstrate that they are good intentioned, not to get property out of your hands and away from creditors.

5. Develop a consistent plan of gifting transfers. Make them small and they will likely be unnoticed. Consider this example: A parent has three children, and for the past five years has given each child $1,000 per year. In the sixth year, the parent is sued. The $15,000 received by the children over the previous five years is free from attack as a fraudulent transfer. Now consider the

protection plan. He or she has not made annual gifts. In the same year that parent is sued and transfers $15,000 to his or her children. If the parent cannot satisfy the creditor's claim, the gift may very well be vulnerable to a claim of fraudulent transfer.

6.   Know your state's statute of limitations for various claims. The statute of limitations is the law that defines when a party's right to pursue a claim has expired. Although the UFCA does not contain a specific statute of limitations, each state enacted its own time limit when it adopted the UFCA. The time to challenge or void a fraudulent conveyance ranges from 3 to 6 years, depending on your state. Should the debtor be in bankruptcy, the Bankruptcy Code establishes the federal statute of limitations. Section 548 of the Bankruptcy Code provides "the trustee may avoid any transfer of an interest of the debtor in property. . . that was made or incurred on or within one year before the date of the filing of the petition. . . ."

Creditors have rights, too. The law of fraudulent conveyance was established to protect creditors. It was initially developed to give a creditor the right to go after property that was moved by the debtor just to avoid collection of the debt. If a transfer is found to be fraudulent, the creditor can continue to go after both the debtor and the transferred property. In essence, this gives the creditor additional property from which to satisfy its claim.

Generally, creditors pursue cost-effective means of collection. It can be expensive and time consuming to pursue a fraudulent transfer claim, and many creditors will back off from this expense. However, some creditors will fight on, regardless of cost. Do not delude yourself into believing a fraudulent transfer will protect your assets. So, for example, I had one client who was willing to pay me $500 to collect a $100 debt. He didn't care a whit about the cost; he simply would not permit a debtor to beat him.

UNIFORM FRAUDULENT CONVEYANCE ACT

Sec. 1. Definition of Terms. In this act "Assets" of a debtor means property not exempt from liability for his debts. To the extent that any property is liable for any debts of the debtor, such property shall be included in his assets.

"Conveyance" includes every payment of money, assignment, release, transfer, lease, mortgage or pledge of tangible or intangible property, and also the creation of any lien or encumbrance.

"Creditor" is a person having any claim, whether matured or unmatured, liquidated or unliquidated, absolute, fixed or contingent.

"Debt" includes any legal liability, whether matured or unmatured, liquidated or unliquidated, absolute, fixed or contingent.

Sec. 2. Insolvency.

(1) A person is insolvent when the present fair salable value of his assets is less than the amount that will be required to pay his probable liability on his existing debts as they become absolute and matured.

(2) In determining whether a partnership is insolvent there shall be added to the partnership property the present fair salable value of the separate assets of each general partner in excess of the amount probably sufficient to meet the claims of his separate creditors, and also the amount of any unpaid subscription to the partnership of each limited partner, provided the present fair salable value of the assets of such limited partner is probably sufficient to pay his debts, including such unpaid subscription.

Sec. 3. Fair Consideration. Fair consideration is given for property, or obligation,

(a) When in exchange for such property, or obligation, as a fair equivalent therefor, and in good faith, property is conveyed or a previous debt is satisfied, or

(b) When such property, or obligation is received in good faith to secure a present advance or antecedent debt in amount not disproportionately small as compared with the value of the property, or obligation obtained.

Sec. 4. Conveyances by Insolvent. Every conveyance made and every obligation incurred by a person who is or will be thereby rendered insolvent is fraudulent as to creditors without regard to his actual intent if the conveyance is made or the obligation is incurred without a fair consideration.

Sec. 5. Conveyances by Persons in Business. Every conveyance made without fair consideration when the person making it is engaged or is about to engage in a business or transaction for which the property remaining in his hands after the conveyance is an unreasonably small capital, is fraudulent as to creditors and as to other persons who become creditors during the continuance of such business or transaction without regard to his actual intent.

Sec. 6. Conveyances by a Person about to Incur Debts. Every conveyance made and every obligation incurred without fair consideration when the person making the conveyance or entering into the obligation intends or believes that he will incur debts beyond his ability to pay as they mature, is fraudulent as to both present and future creditors.

Sec. 7. Conveyance Made with Intent to Defraud. Every conveyance made and every obligation incurred with actual intent, as distinguished from intent presumed in law, to hinder, delay, or defraud either present or future creditors, is fraudulent as to both present and future creditors.

Sec. 8. Conveyance of Partnership Property. Every conveyance of partnership property and every partnership obligation incurred when the partnership is or will be thereby rendered insolvent, is fraudulent as to partnership creditors, if the conveyance is made or obligation is incurred

(a) To a partner, whether with or without a promise by him to pay partnership debts, or

(b) To a person (not a partner) without fair consideration to the partnership as distinguished from consideration to the individual partners.

Sec. 9. Rights of Creditors Whose Claims Have Matured.

(1) Where a conveyance or obligation is fraudulent as to a creditor, such creditor, when his claim has matured, may, as against any person except a purchaser for fair consideration without knowledge of the fraud at the time of the purchase, or one who has derived title immediately from such a purchaser,

(a) Have the conveyance set aside or obligation annulled to the extent necessary to satisfy his claim, or

(b) Disregard the conveyance and attach or levy execution upon the property conveyed.

(2) A purchaser who without actual fraudulent intent has given less than a fair consideration for the conveyance or obligation, may retain the property or obligation as security for repayment.

Sec. 10. Rights of Creditors Whose Claims Have Not Matured. Where a conveyance made or obligation incurred is fraudulent as to a creditor whose claim has not matured he may proceed in a court of competent jurisdiction against any person against whom he could have proceeded had his claim matured, and the court may,

(a) Restrain the defendant from disposing of his property,

(b) Appoint a receiver to take charge of the property,

(c) Set aside the conveyance or annul the obligation, or

(d) Make any order which the circumstances of the case may require.

Sec. 11. Cases Not Provided for in Act. In any case not provided for in the Act the rules of law and equity including the law merchant, and in particular the rules relating to the law of principal and agent, and the effect of fraud, misrepresentation, duress or coercion, mistake, bankruptcy or other invalidating cause shall govern.

Sec. 12. Construction of Act. This Act shall be so interpreted and construed as to effectuate its general purpose to make uniform the law of those states which enact it.

Sec. 13. Name of Act. This Act may be cited as the Uniform Fraudulent Conveyance Act.

Sec. 14. Inconsistent Legislation Repealed. Section ...... are hereby repealed, and all acts or parts of acts inconsistent with this Act are hereby repealed.

Understanding and Coping with Collection Procedures 3

Most people who are at risk of losing their property have multiple debts, such as credit cards and installment loans. This creates an interesting tension among their creditors. In essence, they compete to be the first to take the debtor's property to satisfy their debt. Although many professionals and businesspeople fear the risk posed by a lawsuit seeking catastrophic damages, most debtors simply are overextended.

We live in a society that is driven by easy credit. All one need do is look at newspaper or television advertisements. They readily proclaim easy credit. It is not surprising, therefore, that the financial difficulties threatening most debtors are related to the overextension of credit. It is likely that your situation is a result of "borrowing too much" and not having the ability to stay current in your payment obligations.

If this is the case, your creditors are pressuring you to pay. It is also likely that this pressure is magnified by the fact that you have many separate creditors. They may pursue you with letters and phone calls that threaten to damage your credit rating, or institute a lawsuit against you, or take your property.

Asset protection provides early intervention in order to alleviate this stress. You, therefore, must know what your creditors are allowed to do, in order for you to develop the most appropriate plan. The purpose of any plan is to:

1. Eliminate or lessen the stress.

2. Protect your property from loss.

3. Restructure your payments to levels you can afford or to give you a breathing period during which you can protect your assets.

Creditor Collection Techniques

Creditors are not the bad guys in black hats. They are businesspeople, many of whom are located in your community. They are in business to make money. It is their primary goal to sell and hopefully develop goodwill with you as their customer. Remember the motto "the customer is always right." Creditors will work with you if they believe you are acting in good faith, not just stringing them along. Your continued business and your goodwill are more important than what they may lose should they act inappropriately.

Keep in mind that collection is a cost of business and must be economical. It makes little sense for a business to spend an additional fifty cents to collect a dollar. Many creditors will, after a modest effort to collect a small account receivable, write it off. It does not benefit them to continue to pursue small sums of money. As ironic as it may seem, your small account gives you more clout in compromising the overdue portion of your debt than you would have if you owed a large amount of money.

What are the steps a creditor will take to collect accounts? Usually the first step is the bill itself. Thereafter, you will receive reminder statements. Initially the reminder will be a mild notice that your payment is late. It is written to give the impression that your creditor has assumed that you have only overlooked a late payment. In actuality, it is generated by a computer that generates notices simply by reference to fixed "cutoff" dates. Those accounts that have not yet made a timely payment automatically receive a notice. Generally these notices will prompt payment. Sometimes it may take a second or third reminder, but most people will pay up.

It is after the second or third reminder goes unanswered that credit departments take notice and begin to act. When the third reminder goes out, the payment in question is probably 90 days overdue. Creditors recognize that the longer they delay in pursuing collection the less likelihood they have of collecting. At this point you may be receiving notices on a weekly basis. From the creditor's viewpoint, it is important that they let you know they have not overlooked your debt.

Should these notices prove ineffective, the creditor's collection department may write or call you to ask if there are any problems. Again this is an inoffensive type of contact and is used to show your creditor's concern. With the advent of computerized voice-mail, the telephone call is becoming the contact of choice. It is relatively inexpensive, fast and efficient.

Many credit card companies will use the information they receive during a call to you to judge whether it has become appropriate to cancel your credit card. Remember, credit card companies such as Visa and MasterCard provide no product; they make their money like banks, on the fees they collect. Should they decide you are a bad risk, they will cancel your card in order to limit their risk.

It is important for you to recognize the full importance of the initial phone call from a creditor, particularly credit card companies. They use this call to obtain information that will help them decide whether they can expect payment from you or whether they should turn the account over to a collection agency.

Once your creditor enlists a collection agency, it is no longer concerned about your goodwill or your continued patronage. To the contrary, they only want to cut their losses and receive the maximum they can from you. Your best strategy, even in difficult times, is to try to keep your account from going to a collection agency. In fact, your telephone contact may even tell you that they will not refer the matter to a credit reporting agency if you can make some arrangement.

What Collection Agencies Do

Once your account is referred to a collection agency, a new process begins. You will receive a letter from the agency advising you that they have been retained to collect your debt. The letter will advise you to contact the agency, tell you how much you owe and to whom you owe the money. Under the terms of the Fair Debt Collection Act, the letter will provide you with an opportunity to contest the amount owed. Although it is not a frequent event, many collection departments do make errors and this is your last chance to correct it. Many people will pay the debt after receiving this first letter. The reputation of toughness that most collection agencies enjoy convinces many people to pay up.

After the initial contact, the collection agency will be more aggressive than your creditor in trying to collect the debt. The collection agency is in business to make money, and it only makes money by collecting debts. They have become very efficient at their business. As with your creditor, the initial contacts may be cordial reminders of your legal and moral obligation to pay. Thereafter, the collection agency will be more forceful and threatening in tone. You can expect the frequency of contact and the intimidating nature of the contacts to increase exponentially.

Many collection agencies prefer, after the initial contact letter, to proceed over the telephone. The telephone provides them with the advantages of intimidation and flexibility in exaggerating—factors that may not be "legal". It is easy for you simply to ignore a letter, but many people are simply scared by a voice at the other end of the line. Additionally, it is easier to embarrass a debtor during a telephone call than it is in a letter. At some point, the collection agency will determine whether they can expect you to pay. If the decision goes against you, they will refer the matter to an attorney for legal action. You may even receive a letter demanding payment and warning you that this will be your last opportunity to pay before the matter is referred to an attorney.

Once the attorney has been retained, the matter will again begin anew. Many collection attorneys will try to resolve the matter by a negotiated settlement. That is for a reduced amount. Remember, the attorney, like the collection agency, is paid only for successful collection efforts. Today, attorneys are more aggressive and often proceed directly to court. Should you be sued, immediately seek legal advice. If you ignore the suit, your creditor will obtain a judgment against you.

How the Law Limits Collection Practices

The Fair Debt Collection Practices Act prohibits a debt collector from the following:

1. Communicating "at any unusual time or place or a time or place known or which should be known to be inconvenient to the consumer." In the absence of knowledge of circumstances to the contrary, a debt collector must assume convenient times are limited to the hours between 8 A.M. and 9 P.M.

2. Communicating with you at your place of employment if the debt collector knows or has reason to know that your employer prohibits employees from receiving such communications.

3. Continuing to contact you after receiving written notification from you that you wish him to cease contacting you; in that situation, the debt collector may only:

    a. contact you to say that his efforts to collect have ended;
    b. notify you that specific remedies may be pursued; and,
    c. notify you that a specific remedy is being pursued.

4. Contacting you or others, if he knows you are represented by an attorney.

5. Communicating your debt to other than you, the creditor, your attorney or a credit reporting agency.

The FDCPA specifically addresses the issue of harassment and abuse. Section 1692d provides "A debt collector may not engage in any conduct the natural consequence of which is to harass, oppress, or abuse any person in connection with the collection of a debt. Without limiting the general application of the foregoing, the following conduct is a violation of this section:

"(1) The use or threat of use of violence or other criminal means to harm the physical person, reputation, or property of any person.

"(2) The use of obscene or profane language or language the natural consequence of which is to abuse the hearer or reader.

"(3) The publication of a list of consumers who allegedly refuse to pay debts, except to a consumer reporting agency....

"(4) The advertisement for sale of any debt to coerce payment of the debt."

"(5) Causing a telephone to ring or engaging any person in telephone conversation repeatedly or continuously with intent to annoy, abuse, or harass any person at the called number."

"(6) . . .the placement of telephone calls without meaningful disclosure of the caller's identity."

The FDCPA defines what conduct constitutes unfair practices:

1. Accepting a check post-dated more than five days without written notification to you of their intention to deposit the check. The check may not be deposited with less than three days nor more than ten days written notice to you. (The purpose of this provision is to give you the opportunity to ensure that there are sufficient funds in your checking account when the check is eventually deposited.)

2. Soliciting a post-dated check for the purpose of threatening criminal prosecution.

3. Depositing or threatening to deposit any post-dated check prior to the date on the check.

4. Communicating with a consumer regarding a debt by post card. (This is to ensure your privacy.)

5. Concealing the true purpose of a collect telephone call or collect telegram in order to get you to accept the call or telegram and pay the charges.

6. Using any language or symbol, other than the debt collector's address, on any envelope or telegram if that language or symbol would indicate the correspondence is from a debt collector. (The debt collector may not even use its business name on the envelope if its name would identify it as a debt collector.)

The FDCPA defines what are false or misleading practices. "A debt collector may not use any false, deceptive, or misleading representation or means in connection with the collection of any debt. Without limiting the general application of the foregoing, the following conduct is a violation of this section:

"(1) The false representation or implication that the debt collector is vouched for, bonded by, or affiliated with the United States or any State, including the use of any badge, uniform, or facsimile thereof.

"(2) The false representation of—
    "(A) the character, amount , or legal status of any debt; or
    "(B) any services rendered or compensation which may be lawfully received by any debt collector for the collection of a debt.

"(3) The false representation or implication that any individual is an attorney or that any communication is from an attorney.

"(4) The representation or implication that nonpayment of any debt will result in the arrest or imprisonment of any person or the seizure, garnishment, attachment, or sale of any property or wages of any person unless such action is lawful and the debt collector or creditor intends to take such action.

"(5) The threat to take any action that cannot legally be taken or that is not intended to be taken.

"(6) The false representation or implication

that a sale, referral, or other transfer of any interest in a debt shall cause the consumer to—

"(A) lose any claim or defense to payment of the debt, or

"(B) become the subject to any practice prohibited by this subchapter.

"(7) The false representation or implication that the consumer committed any crime or other conduct in order to disgrace the consumer.

"(8) Communicating or threatening to communicate to any person credit information which is known or which should be known to be false, including the failure to communicate that a disputed debt is disputed.

"(9) The use or distribution of any written communication which simulates or is falsely represented to be a document authorized, issued, or approved by any court, official, or agency of the United States, or any State, or which creates a false impression as to its source, authorization, or approval.

"(10) The use of any false representation or deceptive means to collect or attempt to collect any debt or to obtain information concerning a consumer.

"(11) Except as otherwise provided for communications to acquire location information under section 1692b of this title, the failure to disclose clearly in all communications made to collect a debt, or to obtain information about a consumer, that the debt collector is attempting to collect a debt and that any information obtained will be used for that purpose.

"(12) The false representation or implication that accounts have been turned over to innocent purchasers for value.

"(13) The false representation or implication that documents are legal process.

"(14) The use of any business, company, or organization name other than the true name of the debt collector's business, company or organization.

"(15) The false representation or implication that documents are not legal process forms or do not require legal action by the consumer.

"(16) The false representation or implication that a debt collector operates or is employed by a consumer reporting agency as defined by section 1681a(f) of this title."

If you are faced with what you believe to be a "harassing" collection agency, you can halt their efforts by complaining to the Federal Trade Commission or your state's consumer protection agency. Should you determine that the collector has broken the law, you may now have an effective weapon against the collection effort.

Debt Resolution Without Bankruptcy

Assume your debts exceed your income, or at least your ability to provide for your family's bare necessities if you paid all of your obligations. Collection agencies are likely to be ringing your phone and you have been threatened with losing everything you own. Something has to give. Ultimately you can resolve many of these claims by declaring bankruptcy, but, for a number of reasons, bankruptcy should be a course of last resort. Instead, you should consider the potential of bankruptcy a tool with which you can get your creditors to listen to reason. They know full well that if you do go into bankruptcy, they are unlikely to get more than a few cents of every dollar you owe.

By gently reminding your creditors that you are contemplating bankruptcy, they may become more willing to work with you or give you the time you need to put one or all three of the following options into play:

1.   Consolidate your debts.

2.   Enter into a new installment agreement.

3.   Try to compromise the amount due.

In order to choose the correct strategy or combination of strategies, you need to understand your ability to borrow or make payments. First, you must measure your ability to borrow. The forms that appear at the end of this chapter should prove useful in collecting information and determining your borrowing strength. You must account for all of your cash, stocks, bonds, investments, life insurance, and other property against which you can borrow, particularly real estate. If the total of your available assets is greater than your outstanding debts, then you may be served by a debt consolidation loan.

There is one caution that must be posted: a consolidation loan will enable you to satisfy your current debt—but it will create a new debt that you will have to pay down. You must ensure that the monthly payments on your consolidation loan are meaningfully lower than the total of the payments the loan will satisfy. Do not dig a bigger hole by signing up for a loan that requires monthly payments greater than either your ability to repay or your current monthly payments.

Next, you must measure your income's ability to service your existing debts. To do this, determine your monthly income after deductions for taxes (federal, state and local income, and Social Security) and other withholding items, i.e., union dues, support payments, wage garnishment, medical and/or

life insurance coverage, and I.R.A.s. Now list all of your expenses. Do not be stingy—be realistic as to what you must spend. Do not underestimate costs of food, your mortgage or rent, gasoline, telephone, utilities, and clothing. In addition, make sure you include annual and other installment obligations, such as property taxes, car insurance, school tuition, and water and other utility bills that come due other than monthly. Include these obligations and "budget" a monthly amount for them. Too many debtors ignore the need to set aside this money and break their budget when the semi-annual homeowner's insurance policy premium arrives. They pay that bill but cannot pay the bills for the rest of their necessities for the next several weeks.

Now, subtract your monthly expenses from your "net take home pay". If the number is a positive number, that is your available source of funds for debt reduction. It is the money you will use to repay your overdue and delinquent bills.

If the amount is zero or less, your income alone will not resolve your problem. You should explore the possibility of obtaining a debt consolidation loan, a negotiated installment agreement, or a compromise of your accounts, and, as a last resort, bankruptcy.

If your income will allow you to pay your delinquencies within a year, you have a sporting chance to reach an understanding with your creditors. You will have to be honest, both with yourself and your creditors. If you do not have the income strength to pay off your bills within one year, then some compromise or bankruptcy is in order.

Debt Consolidation Loans

A debt consolidation loan is a single, large borrowing, the proceeds of which are used to pay off a group of smaller loans. Given the nature of the lenders who offer debt consolidation loans, there is a better than average chance that the interest rate you'll have to pay them will be less than the

interest rates associated with charge cards and other consumer loans. A second benefit flows from the fact that your debt consolidation loan can be stretched out over a longer term than most consumer loans. That means you will be paying less to amortize the loan each month.

There is a tradeoff here. You will ultimately pay more in interest on a debt consolidation loan since it runs for a longer term than your consumer loans. But, you'll be paying less each month, and that can help you work out of a difficult situation.

Shopping for a Debt Consolidation Loan

Start with family. Although you may think it humiliating, families do tend to try to protect their own. If your family members have the financial wherewithal, they may be willing to pull you out of your difficulties. Or, instead of lending the money directly to you, your family may be willing to use its cash as collateral for a loan from your credit union or bank. Loans backed by certificates of deposit, for example, receive the most favorable interest rates available. Lastly, there are the finance companies. They are generally the least discriminating lenders. However, they will charge a fairly high interest rate, and you should compare their monthly payment requirements to your existing payment totals.

Second, or home equity, loans have become a popular tool for financing. The home equity loan "converts" the equity you have in your home to cash. This pool of cash may be enough for you to pay off your debts. Even if you have a bad credit history, do not be afraid to pursue a home equity loan. You'll be offering sound collateral (your home), and you may be able to get a meaningfully lower interest rate than the rate charged by finance companies.

TRAP: Do not over-leverage your home. For example, at a time when the current real estate market is poor, your property may actually lose value during the course of your home equity loan. Make certain the loan agreement does not require your home to maintain a certain value, or you may be forced to repay a portion of the loan earlier than you expected.

If you are a participant in a pension plan, you may have an excellent source of capital. Find out if your pension plan was structured to allow you to borrow against it. A pension is permitted by law to loan money to participants, but does not have to do so unless the terms of the plan allow borrowing. The law permits pension plans to loan money to plan participants subject to the following provisions: you can borrow at the least $10,000, and not more than $50,000; amounts between those two figures can be loaned if they do not exceed one-half of your vested account balance. The loan must be repaid within five years, but can be written for a longer term if it is collateralized with a mortgage on real property.

Lastly, review your life insurance policies. Many policies provide a "cash value" against which you can borrow. If your policy is new, this amount may be minimal. On older policies the cash surrender value may be substantial.

Selling Assets to Raise Money

You may choose to sell some of your belongings to raise money. If so, try to follow these rules:

1. Be realistic in determining the value of your property. Your "customers" know they are not shopping in a store that handles new merchandise. They may also suspect that you are selling under distress.

2. Try to sell property that has high value or desirability.

3. Sell only items that you will not have to replace.

4. Try not to be emotional, even if the property you have to put up for sale holds an emotional attachment for you. The relief from the stress created by your creditors will usually overcome the sentimental attachment you have for that family heirloom.

5. If possible, return their property to creditors who are pressing you. Make certain to obtain a release. This will absolve you of any of the outstanding debt on the original transaction. Should you not get a release, your creditor will come after you for the difference between the amount you owed and the value of the returned property.

Assuming these options are available to you, you should be able to work your way free from your debt problems. If you do, keep this sad fact of life in mind: many people who are newly debt free act like alcoholics and go back to their old habits. In no time they are deeply in debt, but now they have fewer assets with which to work their way out of trouble. There are just so many times a house can be mortgaged.

The way to get out of debt and stay out of debt is to operate religiously within the confines of a budget. This does not mean you have no leeway for discretionary spending. It does mean that you must be disciplined in your spending.

Develop Your Extended Payment Schedule

Assume you've done all that you can. You have sold all nonessential property, remortgaged your home, and tried unsuccessfully to borrow from every conceivable source. You've come up short, and your creditors are still hounding you.

Do not despair; there are still two options you can consider. Using the creditor's fear that you may file for bankruptcy protection, you may be able to get your creditors to agree to an extended repayment schedule.

The benefit to extended repayment plans is that they allow you to reduce the amount of your monthly payments. If you have a regular income stream, you should try to reach an extended payment plan with your creditors. Most creditors fear bankruptcy as they know they will generally get only pennies on the dollar. An extended plan offers them the chance to get full payment, albeit later than expected.

The Two Types of Extended Plans

There are two forms of extended payment plans that are not within bankruptcy: self-administered and credit counselor plans.

In a self-administered approach, you contact your creditors. You offer the terms with the threat of bankruptcy in the background. Many times this is enough to be successful. I recently met with a client who owed about $10,000 in unsecured debt. He wanted to declare bankruptcy. However, he had a steady job and did have about $300 a month to put towards bills. We contacted all of his creditors. This did two things. First, it took the collection agency off his case

because he followed the FDCPA and told them to stop contacting him. Second, the creditors were notified that we were attempting in good faith to resolve his financial difficulties. Most creditors readily consented to a three-year repayment plan, once they recognized they were all being treated equally. The few creditors that tried to take a hard line backed down when faced with the prospect that my client could offer no other option than filing for bankruptcy.

As discussed above, this approach requires you to make a realistic budget and have a firm handle on your ability to pay. In effect, you will be entering into a new contract with all of your creditors. Treat all of them equally and the strategy should be successful. However, you must be able to live with your agreement, because you will not get a second chance.

The second non-bankruptcy approach calls for you to use a credit counseling service sponsored by your local consumer credit counseling service. This is a more formalized approach than the self-administered plan. Creditors favor this approach since you agree to turn over your paycheck to the credit service. The service gives you an "allowance" to live on and uses the rest of your paycheck to service your debt. Most creditors are willing to trust a consumer credit service to verify that your plan is fair and honest.

Both of these approaches require you to be open about your situation. At the end of this chapter, you will find a model letter you can use to propose an extended debt repayment plan. Look it over carefully. You will see that you should not hide your difficulties, but own up to them and rely on the good judgment of your creditor to work the problem out with you.

Here are some things to look out for:

1. Make sure your arrangement is in writing. Your worst nightmare could come to life if you proceed to make payments and then suddenly end up on the receiving end of a lawsuit thrown at you by a disgruntled creditor. If the agreement is in writing, you have a contract that will protect you from such sneak attacks.

2. Wait until you get all of your creditors in line. Why pay before you have an agreement with all of your creditors?. You want this to be a productive arrangement. If less than all creditors eventually accept your plan, the non-consenting creditors may end up forcing you into bankruptcy.

3. Make the acceptance of the program a condition to your beginning it. Require at least an 85% participation of your unsecured creditors. This may exert enough pressure for all of your unsecured creditors to sign up.

4. If possible, do not sign away any of your legal rights. Many creditors will request that you consent to a confession of judgment to them as part of the agreement. A confession of judgment would allow a creditor to get a judgment against you simply by filing the confession with the court. You are precluded from defending the claim. In some states this is impermissible. Check your state's laws.

Compromise the Claim

A compromise agreement usually provides the last opportunity you and your creditors will have to resolve your debt problems short of a lawsuit or a bankruptcy filing. In effect, you are pre-negotiating a bankruptcy result. You will educate your creditors to the fact that you have very little equity, so that they will understand it will not be fruitful for them to sue you, and that you are willing to give them at least what they would get if you declared bankruptcy.

A compromise requires you to be fair and equitable with your creditors. Try to provide an up-front cash payment and some form of payout with which you can live.

A compromise agreement is a contract that binds you and your creditors. A model compromise agreement is printed at the end of this chapter. You may negotiate with any of your creditors, but, unless you enlist your largest creditors, you will be unable to enlist the others. You must negotiate in good faith.

Reaching a compromise on your debts requires both you and your creditors to be flexible. Keep in mind the fact that creditors only want their money.

What Will You Offer?

Be fair, but start on the low side. Do not make your best offer—this is a horse swap, not a retail purchase. Increase your offer in modest amounts. Do not let your creditors bully you. You know that in the worst situation you can always go bankrupt and be no worse off.

When Should You Pay?

Offer what you can afford as an up front payment. Do not offer more than you will have available in the future. Do not project possible increases in income when you make your offer. Work with what you are making today since you have no guarantee that you will be earning more in the future.

How Long Should the Compromise Last?

Try not to permit the compromise agreement to set a term of more than two years. Never agree to one that exceeds three years. Even bankruptcy only requires you to pay out over a three-year schedule. If faced with a creditor unwilling to compromise on time, let him face you in bankruptcy. He will not get more from you in bankruptcy than through a compromise agreement, and he knows that for a fact.

Should You Return Property?

Maybe. Property has value, and the basis of your debt is value. Negotiate the best exchange price and try to get a release for the deficiency.

Should You Pay Interest on the Outstanding Balance?

Your creditor will expect interest to be paid. Often the interest charge is what got you in trouble initially. Try not to agree to pay interest. As you will see in Chapter 5, creditors do not receive interest in bankruptcy; if your creditor does not know this, educate him.

Can You Protect Your Credit Rating?

You may be able to negotiate a good record from a creditor, once you've established a track record of timely payments in conformity with your agreement. This is subject to mutual agreement and you will probably have to push for it. But, it is worth fighting for, since it provides you with a tool to rehabilitate a bad credit history.

Your Best Selling Points

You must convince your creditors that it is in their best interest to come to an agreement with you outside of bankruptcy. Stress the following:

1. Regular payments are better than no payments.

2. The compromise will enable your creditor to avoid the use of a collection agency or lawyer—options that can cost up to twenty-five percent of the amount they collect.

3. You are not a dead beat looking to "beat" the system. You have come forward in a sincere manner at a difficult time. You are entitled to be treated with respect.

4. You are trying to avoid bankruptcy. As previously stated, many bankruptcies result in less than five cents on the dollar being paid to creditors. Your creditor knows this and should be willing to compromise, particularly if it appears he will be getting more than he would in a bankruptcy. Remember, while you may be able to file for bankruptcy without a lawyer, if your creditor is a corporation it must be represented by a lawyer. Legal costs can eat up virtually all of the return a creditor receives from a bankrupt's estate.

For all of the above reasons, a sensible creditor should be willing to enter into an agreement with you.

DEBTOR PROTECTION FORMS

Outstanding Debt (Include Credit Card Debt)

Creditor:	Total Debt	Amount Paid	Amount Outstanding	Due Date
MORTGAGES:				
_____	_____	_____	_____	_____
_____	_____	_____	_____	_____
AUTOMOBILE LOANS:				
_____	_____	_____	_____	_____
_____	_____	_____	_____	_____
CREDIT CARDS:				
_____	_____	_____	_____	_____
_____	_____	_____	_____	_____
_____	_____	_____	_____	_____
REVOLVING CREDIT:				
_____	_____	_____	_____	_____
_____	_____	_____	_____	_____
_____	_____	_____	_____	_____
OTHER LOANS:				
_____	_____	_____	_____	_____
_____	_____	_____	_____	_____
_____	_____	_____	_____	_____
UNPAID TAXES:				
_____	_____	_____	_____	_____
_____	_____	_____	_____	_____
_____	_____	_____	_____	_____
_____	_____	_____	_____	_____
_____	_____	_____	_____	_____

Net Assets Available for Borrowing

Asset:	Current Fair Market Value	Current Loans Against Asset	Net Equity
REAL PROPERTY:			
_____	$ _____	$ _____	$ _____
_____	$ _____	$ _____	$ _____
AUTOMOBILES:			
_____	$ _____	$ _____	$ _____
_____	$ _____	$ _____	$ _____
MARKETABLE SECURITIES:			
_____	$ _____	$ _____	$ _____
_____	$ _____	$ _____	$ _____
_____	$ _____	$ _____	$ _____
_____	$ _____	$ _____	$ _____
PERSONAL PROPERTY:			
_____	$ _____	$ _____	$ _____
_____	$ _____	$ _____	$ _____
_____	$ _____	$ _____	$ _____
_____	$ _____	$ _____	$ _____
_____	$ _____	$ _____	$ _____
_____	$ _____	$ _____	$ _____
LIFE INSURANCE (Cash Surrender Value):			
_____	$ _____	$ _____	$ _____
_____	$ _____	$ _____	$ _____
_____	$ _____	$ _____	$ _____
_____	$ _____	$ _____	$ _____
_____	$ _____	$ _____	$ _____

Bare Necessity Schedule

Month: _____

Rent/Mortgage $_____

Food $_____

Clothing $_____

Utilities (Gas, Electric, Telephone, Water) $_____

Transportation (Gas, Auto Payments,
    Public Transportation) $_____

Insurance (Auto, Life, Health, Medical) $_____

Uninsured Medical (Dental, Medicines, etc.) $_____

Educational Expenses $_____

Miscellaneous:

_____ $_____

_____ $_____

_____ $_____

_____ $_____

_____ $_____

_____ $_____

_____ $_____

TOTAL BARE NECESSITY EXPENSES $ _____

Current Income after Withholding and Deductions $ _____

Amount Available for Debt Reduction: $ _____
(If Bare Necessity expenses exceed Net Income,
 enter the total as a negative number)

Proposed Debt Payment Plan

Creditor	Total Amount Owed	Current Monthly Payment	Proposed Monthly Payment
_____	$ _____	$ _____	$ _____
_____	$ _____	$ _____	$ _____
_____	$ _____	$ _____	$ _____
_____	$ _____	$ _____	$ _____
_____	$ _____	$ _____	$ _____
_____	$ _____	$ _____	$ _____
_____	$ _____	$ _____	$ _____
_____	$ _____	$ _____	$ _____
_____	$ _____	$ _____	$ _____
_____	$ _____	$ _____	$ _____
_____	$ _____	$ _____	$ _____
_____	$ _____	$ _____	$ _____
_____	$ _____	$ _____	$ _____
_____	$ _____	$ _____	$ _____
_____	$ _____	$ _____	$ _____
_____	$ _____	$ _____	$ _____
_____	$ _____	$ _____	$ _____
_____	$ _____	$ _____	$ _____
_____	$ _____	$ _____	$ _____
_____	$ _____	$ _____	$ _____
_____	$ _____	$ _____	$ _____
_____	$ _____	$ _____	$ _____
_____	$ _____	$ _____	$ _____
_____	$ _____	$ _____	$ _____

PROPOSAL SEEKING AN OUT-OF-COURT SETTLEMENT

(Date)

Mr. John Collection
Credit Manager
Creditor Corporation
123 Market Street
Collection City, FL, 00000

Account Number:

Dear Mr. Collection:

As you may know, I have fallen behind in making my monthly payments on the above-referenced account. Quite simply, my employer closed its doors three months ago, and I have been forced to accept a new position that pays less than seventy-five percent of the salary I earned with my former employer.

Attached to this letter you will find three schedules. The first attachment is a schedule that sets out both my monthly budget for bare necessities and, additionally, the amount I have left over from my net take-home pay after paying for those necessities. At the present time, I take home less than $100 above the amount I need for necessities.

The second attachment lists all of my creditors, the amount owed to each, and the current monthly payment I am obligated to make to each creditor. As the schedule indicates, my monthly obligations to my creditors is $2,100, well above the $100 I have available. Even if all of my creditors were willing to grant me extended payback terms, it is clear that I simply do not have enough income to offer a realistic payback program.

The third attachment lists the assets against which I can borrow. Based on that schedule, I believe I can raise enough money to pay each of my creditors thirty-five percent of the money I owe them, if each creditor is willing to accept such a payment as full satisfaction of the amount owed. This offer is being made on the same terms to every creditor listed on the second attachment (entitled Outstanding Debt). If accepted by my creditors, I will begin liquidating my assets and will make payment to all of my creditors no later than (date).

I recognize only too well that I am asking my creditors to suffer a loss of 65 cents on every dollar I owe. Frankly, I have no other option. From my creditors' point of view, I believe this proposal is more attractive than a forced bankruptcy which would probably provide as little as pennies for each dollar owed.

If the plan I have proposed is agreeable to Collection Corporation, please sign below under the words "Agreed and Accepted" and return the original copy of this letter.

Sincerely,

Phillip Debtor

Agreed and Accepted:

_____

Date:

AGREEMENT EXTENDING DEBT REPAYMENT

FOR VALUE RECEIVED, the Creditor Company, a corporation organized under the laws of the State of Delaware, hereinafter referred to as "Collection" and John Debtor, hereinafter referred to as "Debtor", agree to the following:

ONE: Under the terms of an agreement dated the first day of April, 19   , Debtor owes $3,000.00 to Creditor.

TWO: The above mentioned $3,000.00 was due and payable to Creditor on the first day of June, 19   , and such payment is now ninety days overdue.

THREE: Debtor is not capable of paying the $3,000 at this time.

FOUR: In consideration of Creditor's willingness to extend the time and manner in which the debt is to be repaid, Debtor hereby agrees to make payment on the following dates and in the following amounts:

Date	Amount
October 1, 19	$1,000.00
November 1, 19	$1,000.00
December 1, 19	$1,000.00

FIVE: Should Debtor fail to make any of the above extended payments on the dates shown above, he shall forfeit all of his rights under this agreement and Creditor shall be entitled to demand the entire amount outstanding on the date of the default and to proceed to collect such sum. Should Debtor default and Creditor find it necessary to employ an attorney to collect all sums outstanding after the default, Debtor agrees to pay all costs of collection, including reasonable attorneys' fees.

Signed this   day of   , 19   .

_____
Creditor

_____
Debtor

(Corporate Seal(s) if either or both parties are corporations)

PROPOSAL TO CREDITORS
SEEKING EXTENDED REPAYMENT PROGRAM

(Date)

Mr. John Collection
Credit Manager
Creditor Corporation
123 Market Street
Collection City, FL, 00000

Account Number:

Dear Mr. Collection:

As you may know, I have fallen behind in making my monthly payments on the above-referenced account. Quite simply, my employer closed its doors three months ago, and I have been forced to accept a new position that pays less than seventy five percent of the salary I earned with my former employer.

I now find myself unable to pay my various debts in a timely fashion. My current earnings will enable me to meet my obligations, but only if my various creditors are willing to extend the length of my debt by lowering the amount of my monthly payments.

In order to assist you in evaluating my request, I have included two documents as an attachment to this letter. The first attachment is a schedule that sets out both my monthly budget for bare necessities and, additionally, the amount I have left over from my net take-home pay after paying for those necessities. At the present time, I take home $650.00 above the amount I need for necessities.

The second attachment lists all of my creditors, the amount owed to each, the current monthly payment I am obligated to make to each creditor, and the amount I propose to make to each creditor.

As the second schedule makes clear, I do not propose to favor any one creditor. Each would receive the same percentage of the $650.00 I have available that their credit beats to my total debt. Under my proposal, I would make monthly payments of $35 to the Creditor Corporation.

As you review the two attachments to this letter, I am certain you will find that my proposal is being made in the utmost of good faith. I am sincerely committed to paying my debts in full, and I know that if you will work with me, your company will be paid in full. I also know that the plan I have proposed sets out the best possible approach to my current problems. The only other option would call for my creditors to force me into bankruptcy, a course of action that would result in my creditors receiving only a few cents on the dollars I owe them.

If the plan I have proposed is agreeable to Collection Corporation, please sign below under the words "Agreed and Accepted" and return the original copy of this letter. I will start making payments under this proposal on the first business day of the month following the date you indicate your acceptance of my proposal.

Sincerely,

Phillip Debtor

Agreed and Accepted:

_____

Date:

FORMAL AGREEMENT COMPROMISING A DEBT

FOR VALUE RECEIVED, the Creditor Company, a corporation organized under the laws of the State of Delaware, hereinafter referred to as "Collection" and John Debtor, hereinafter referred to as "Debtor", agree to the following:

ONE: Under the terms of an agreement dated the first day of April, 19 , Debtor owes $3,000.00 to Creditor.

TWO: The above mentioned $3,000.00 was due and payable to Creditor on the first day of June, 19 , and such payment is now ninety days overdue.

THREE: Debtor is not capable of paying the $3,000.00 at this time.

FOUR: In consideration of Creditor's willingness to accept a total of $1,500.00 in full satisfaction of the $3,000.00 owed by Debtor, Debtor hereby agrees to make three payments of $500.00 each on the following dates:

> October 1, 19
> November 1, 19
> December 1, 19

FIVE: Should Debtor fail to make any of the above payments on the dates shown above, he shall forfeit all of his rights under this agreement and Creditor shall be entitled to demand the entire $3,000.00 that was outstanding prior to the date of this agreement less any payments made by Debtor subsequent to the signing of this agreement. Should Debtor default and Creditor find it necessary to employ an attorney to collect all sums outstanding after the default, Debtor agrees to pay all costs of collection, including reasonable attorneys' fees.

Signed this   day of   , 19   .

_____
Creditor

_____
Debtor

(Corporate Seal(s) if either or both parties are corporations)

Secured Liens, Repossession and IRS Tax Seizures

4

Dealing With Secured Creditors

The creditor with the strongest claim against you is your secured creditor, e.g., the bank that holds the mortgage on your home or the lender who has a lien against the title of your car. The strength of these creditors comes from the fact that they, by virtue of their secured interest, already have a hook into your property, at least the part that is secured. Delinquency on these obligations can more quickly result in your losing the property that secures the loan. Look at all of the banks and savings and loans that are being taken over by the government. New regulations require the lending institutions to act more quickly when a debtor defaults on his loan. As a result, it is more difficult to negotiate a problem loan.

Lenders actually do not want to foreclose on property. Banks are not in the real estate business. More often than not, a bank loses money when it forecloses on a parcel of property. The rash of failed banks can be traced in large part to the issuance of loans that went bad, with the result that banks ended up with non-income producing property. Remember, banks are in the business of making money by loaning money; they are not in the business of brokering real estate or, even worse, becoming landlords.

In addition, banks do not want to show their shareholders that they are poor judges of credit. Loans on which they must foreclose hurt their financial performance and sometimes cause bank officers to lose their jobs.

Just because the lender may not want to foreclose does not mean it will not do so. The bank's position is as "protected" as possible by virtue of the fact that it is a secured creditor. You must deal with the bank on its terms. However, if the lender is not unreasonable, your good faith effort, coupled with an open and frank disclosure of your situation, may turn your lender around and give it a basis upon which to work with you instead of against you.

The Threat of Foreclosure

If you are in arrears in your mortgage, both you and the bank will know it. Typically you receive monthly notices if your mortgage payment is late. Go two or three months without a payment and you will receive both late notices and telephone calls from the bank's customer service department. *Do not ignore these calls.* Responding to them in an effective way will be the first line of defense in your efforts to avoid foreclosure. It is at this time that you will have your first opportunity to negotiate and hold off any further formal foreclosure proceedings.

This first attempt at collection by the bank will give you a chance to explain your plight. For example, you may have recently been laid off. Often the bank is understanding and may agree to pursue one or more of the following alternatives:

1. *Check your spending habits.* The first payments that should be made, after food, are your mortgage payments. Many people get into difficulty by spending on non-necessities. While it may call for belt tightening and may make some unsecured creditors unhappy, paying your mortgage will protect both your family and your most important asset—your home.

2. *Provide a moratorium on payments for a short while.* In essence, the bank is delaying the payment obligation while you get your financial situation improved. This is generally a short-term stoppage of payments and requires you to demonstrate to the bank's satisfaction that there is enough value in your home to justify a moratorium.

3. *Arrange to pay only interest.* Again this is a short-term option, one that will run no more than six months. It generally does not require the bank to make sure there is sufficient equity. The payment of interest provides a benefit to the bank; it can at least show income on the loan. A non-performing loan looks far worse on the bank's financial reports than a loan that makes regular interest payments. While this strategy can save you some money, be careful. The payments on newer mortgages are mostly interest, so the savings may be minor. If your mortgage is older, then most of the payments will reduce the outstanding principal. You are more likely to get an interest-only plan if your mortgage is newer. You might have better luck renegotiating an older mortgage since you will have more equity in the property if you've been paying down the mortgage for a number of years.

If none of these alternatives proves viable, do not wait. Seek out the services of an attorney who specializes in either real estate or bankruptcy. If your lawyer negotiates on your behalf before formal foreclosure proceedings begin, he or she may be able to turn the bank around, particularly if the bank did not believe you or have faith in your promises.

Some alternatives that may be successful prior to a foreclosure being completed are:

1. *Refinance your current mortgage.* Since the early 1980s, mortgage rates have fluctuated and have been rising in recent years. Your problems might stem from a high mortgage rate. My first rate was 14%. I successfully refinanced at 9.5% and reduced my monthly payments by more than $300. This is not always an easy route to follow. Your credit might have already been damaged to the point where you cannot refinance for any savings. However, try; without trying you will already have lost!

2. *Obtain a home equity loan.* Also known as a second mortgage, a home equity loan may provide you with the flexibil-

ity you need to "catch up" on your first mortgage. As noted with the payment moratorium, you must have enough value in your home to get such a mortgage. In general, a second mortgage company will lend up to 75% or 80% of the value of your home minus the already outstanding mortgage.

BEWARE: A second mortgage is also a secured loan. Do not fall into the trap of repairing the first mortgage and falling behind on the second mortgage. Should you fall into arrears on the second mortgage, you could lose your home—the second mortgagee can also foreclose if you do not meet your payment obligations. If this happens, you will only have delayed the situation instead of correcting it.

3. Change your interest rate. This is similar to refinancing your mortgage. If you have an old mortgage, many banks would prefer to "mark up" the interest rate to current market rates. The resetting of your interest rate will probably cost you less than refinancing, and may make the bank more willing to see you through a short-term difficulty.

4. Offer an "equity" interest. This calls for you to offer to make the bank a partner in the value of your home. Not only will you make payments to the bank, but when you sell the property they will receive a percentage of the proceeds—over and above the outstanding mortgage amount. This option is generally used in the context of commercial real estate, but you may be able to convince the bank to adopt it for residential real estate.

5. Convert to negative amortization. This strategy adds any unpaid amounts to the balance that will be owed at the end of the mortgage term. Many variable rate mortgages contain a negative amortization provision.

6. If you are elderly, consider a negative mortgage. Similar to a negative amortization, a negative mortgage pays you

monthly, and the bank recoups its loan to you when you die and your house is sold. This is generally only a good idea for elderly people who NEED the income, not to protect the house from foreclosure.

What if your situation is desperate and the bank will not accept any of the above options? Consider the following:

1. Collateralize your loan with more property. If you have any other property of value, offer it as additional collateral. This may give you enough "equity" in property to successfully renegotiate or refinance your mortgage.

2. Get a co-signer or guarantor. If your credit is not strong enough, maybe the additional strength of a co-signer/guarantor will get you past the bank's objections. In effect, your co-signer is on the hook should you default. You must therefore have a strong relationship with whomever you approach to co-sign/guarantee for you.

3. Consider moving. Before foreclosure, you own your home. The bank only has a lien against it for the value of the mortgage. If you cannot pay the mortgage, you may be in over your head. Selling, even in today's bad market, will bring you more money than you will get if the bank forecloses. Forced sales always result in depressed prices.

4. Have your attorney carefully review your loan agreements. Although it is unlikely that the agreement was not properly drafted, an error can give you quite a bit of leverage. Many states have usury laws. If a loan is deemed to be usurious, the lender will not be able to collect any payment and may ultimately be responsible to you for penalties. So, for example, I'm aware of a New Jersey situation in which the bank was forced to provide a below prime rate loan due to a drafting error in the mortgage.

5. Consider bankruptcy. Once an individ-

ual files for bankruptcy, a foreclosure cannot proceed without bankruptcy court approval. Bankruptcy can provide you with the time you need to catch up. See Chapter 5 for a fuller explanation of why bankruptcy is a valuable option that you should not overlook, particularly if you believe—incorrectly—that

persons who file for bankruptcy are stigmatized.

One final word—if you fall behind, the day is not lost. If you act promptly and maintain open, good faith lines of communication with your lender, you are more likely to succeed than you are to fail in your efforts to save your home.

Protecting Other Property

It should not surprise you when you learn that creditors use the same strategies to collect debts for personal property that they employ in connection with secured property. Creditors know that a delinquent debt becomes a questionable collection the longer it goes unpaid. As a result, in today's economy collection agencies and departments move quickly to collect past due debts.

Banks and finance companies frequently subscribe to credit bureaus to keep track of clients who may be poor payers. When your payments are late, credit bureaus make this information known to their subscribers. Generally, secured creditors only concern themselves with your payment on their property and the equity they have in the property. This is changing with all of the bankruptcies today. Many creditors will act swiftly to reduce their losses and may contact you more quickly about late payments than they did in the past.

As I advised with respect to mortgage problems, one option open to you is to refinance your loan. Many finance companies will offer this opportunity to "catch up". Be careful! The only concerns finance companies have is making money. They will look to your ability to pay and whether you have enough value in your property to protect their interests. Should you decide to refinance, make sure that you are not just digging a deeper hole by agreeing to a monthly payment you cannot make.

As discussed above, communication is the key. The better you keep your creditors advised of your situation and the more good

faith you show in paying the debt, the more receptive they will be to working out a new payment program. Further, if you show some attempt to make payments—even as low as $25.00 a month—you can keep some of your creditors off your back.

Many of the strategies discussed above can be successful in working out your difficulties with creditors of personal property purchases.

Should you be unsuccessful in negotiating a payout, you may be faced with the threat of repossession of your property. In most states repossession is regulated by the Uniform Commercial Code. The UCC provides the following for repossessions that are not ordered by a court:

1.   Creditors may repossess property without court approval if it can be done in a peaceful fashion. Car repossessors can take your car faster than a thief. They will take it under this provision of the UCC in situations that fall just short of a taking at gun point. Do not be surprised if you go shopping and come out of the store to find that your car has disappeared.

2.   You are entitled to any profit on the sale of your property. Let's assume your car was repossessed. If your loan was for $5,000 and the sale of the car was for $7,000, then the finance company must give you $2,000 minus the cost of the repossession and sale. This, however, is often more cold comfort than actual result since forced sales rarely bring the true value of an item.

More often than not, the debtor is left without a car and without any income from the sale.

3. You have the right to "redeem" your property by paying the full amount due on the loan plus expenses of repossession. This is all your creditor really wants. Most finance companies and banks are not in the car or boat or secured property business. Often they lose money when they have to sell property to satisfy the debt.

The tools available to the IRS are coveted by all other debt collectors. As tough as most collection agencies seem, the IRS can get even tougher. The IRS has the ability, without court action, to seize and take your property to satisfy a tax obligation. Its most used tool is the seizure right. This means that without prior notice to you they can grab your bank accounts and freeze them. Imagine what will happen when you start bouncing checks all around town because the IRS has seized your bank account! Seizure is also the IRS's tool of last resort. The primary strategy you must employ to prevent the IRS from seizing your property should involve a combination of cooperation and communication.

As with all creditors, communication is the key to avoiding a seizure of property. The IRS is particularly receptive to requests to work out an arrangement. But it can't agree to a workout unless you speak with them. A quick response to an IRS letter is likely to stop a seizure from occurring.

The first step in the IRS collection process calls for the Service to send you computer bills and notices. Tough collection does not occur until you hear from a collection agent or receive a "Past Due Final Notice" bill from the IRS. But prompt action

The Uniform Commercial Code requires a debtor to sell repossessed property at a reasonable sale price. Should property be sold at a "commercially unreasonable" price, you may be able to sue the creditor and receive money damages. This is not an easy task since you must show that the creditor did not act in good faith. Remember, you are the person who did not make timely payments of your bills, and it will not be hard for the creditor to paint you as the "bad guy."

The IRS—Your Toughest Creditor

Often a seizure results from a taxpayer's refusal to respond or cooperate with the IRS. This may be through ignorance or lack of understanding of the severity of the IRS's collection activities. IF YOU RECEIVE COMMUNICATION FROM THE INTERNAL REVENUE SERVICE, IT IS IMPORTANT THAT YOU PROMPTLY RESPOND AND KEEP A RECORD OF YOUR RESPONSE.

The Internal Revenue Code created a system of voluntary compliance for the payment of taxes. The Internal Revenue Manual provides the procedures a collection agent must comply with before acting to seize your property.

The IRS Seizure Procedure

and response will stop this from occurring. The IRS has been charged to give you every reasonable chance to pay your taxes. The Internal Revenue Manual states, "Procedures are designed (except in jeopardy cases) to give taxpayers a reasonable chance to settle their tax liabilities voluntarily before the more drastic enforcement actions are started." [IRM 5311(3)]

The Internal Revenue Code mandates that notice of intent to seize or levy be delivered in person, at your home, place of business or by registered mail to your last "known" address. Section 6331 of the Internal Revenue Code directs that the "Past Due Final Notice" be sent prior to seizing your accounts or garnishing your wages. This notice will state that if you do not pay within ten days, the Internal Revenue Service will begin collection action.

TRAP: Do not believe that if you do not receive the notice that the IRS cannot proceed. A mailing to your last known address satisfies the Service's good faith requirement. It is your obligation to notify the IRS of a change of address. This is normally done by changing your address on your next tax return. If you are someone who does not file tax returns, you will not be protected should the IRS fail to "track you down." To the contrary, their seizure is likely to be held to be valid.

Usually, the next step involves a call from a collection agent. This will not always occur—particularly if your debt is small. Like other collection agencies, the IRS collection agent will take a tough line with you to get you to pay up or at least enter into a payment plan. Do not take this matter lightly. Your response to the agent at this point will dictate how the IRS proceeds against you—harshly or cooperatively.

Seizing your bank accounts or garnishing your wages is comparatively easy for the IRS and is usually the first attack used by the collection agent. It requires only the filing of a Notice of Levy with your bank or your employer. The IRS will now have your undivided attention—particularly when you bounce a check or get less on pay day.

Taking other property is a bit more complicated for the IRS. First, the Collection Officer must conclude that he must seize property to satisfy the tax obligation. As noted above, your willingness to cooperate shapes the Collection Officer's thinking. At this point, you are inventory in the Collection Officer's files. The IRS likes to move inventory. If you are uncooperative, they will move swiftly to move you, i.e., a seizure. But, if the Collection Officer believes you are acting in good faith, he is likely to grant an extension in order to work out a payment program—even one that compromises your bill.

Should the Collection Officer decide to seize, he will determine which property should be taken. The IRS's policy is not to take property if your equity in it will not generate enough proceeds to cover the costs of the sale. All other property that is not exempt from attachment is likely to be seized or levied against.

How is equity determined? Just take the expected sales price and subtract any secured amounts you owe against the property. The best example is your home. If you owe $80,000 in mortgages and your home is worth $120,000, your equity is $40,000. Similarly, if you owe $7,500 on your car and it is now worth $5,000, you have negative equity of $2,500. In this illustration the IRS would levy against your home but not your car, since the car would not bring in enough to cover the costs of the sale.

Recovering Your Property After an IRS Seizure

There are various ways to have your seized property returned to you. The quickest, but maybe not the least painful, is to pay the tax liability in full. Also, the IRS must return your property once the tax liability becomes unenforceable. Other avenues for release are discretionary with the IRS personnel.

Section 6343 of the Internal Revenue Code authorizes the release of property to the taxpayer if "release of such levy will facilitate the collection of such liability." The regulations issued by the Secretary provide the following conditions of release:

"[T]he district director may release the levy as authorized under subparagraph (1) of this paragraph, if:

"(i) Escrow arrangement. The delinquent taxpayer offers a satisfactory arrangement, which is accepted by the district director, for placing property in escrow to secure the payment of the liability (including expenses of levy) which is the basis of the levy. [This is usually done with either stocks and bonds or business property. It requires you to place the property in the hands of an independent party who "protects" the IRS's interest while allowing you the benefit and use of the property.]

"(ii) Bond. The delinquent taxpayer delivers an acceptable bond to the district director conditioned upon the payment of the liability (including expenses of levy) which is the basis of the levy. Such bond shall be in the form provided in Section 7101 and Section 301.7101-1.

"(iii) Payment of amount of United States' interest in the property. There is paid to the district director an amount determined by him to be equal to the interest of the United States in the seized property or the part of the seized property to be released." [This requires either the payment of the bill in full or entering into an installment payment plan.]

"(iv) Assignment of salaries and wages. The delinquent taxpayer executes an agreement directing his employer to pay to the district director amounts deducted from the employee's wages on a regular, continuing, or periodic basis, in such manner and in such amount as is agreed upon with the district director, until the full amount of the liability is satisfied, and such agreement is accepted by the employer. [This is little more than a negotiated garnishment of your paycheck.]

"(v) Installment Payment arrangement. The delinquent taxpayer makes satisfactory arrangements with the district director to pay the amount of liability in installments.

"(vi) Extension of statute of limitations. The delinquent taxpayer executes an agreement to extend the statute of limitations in accordance with Section 6502(a)(2) and Regulation 301.6502-1.

"(vii) Release where the value of interest of United States is insufficient to meet expenses of sale. The district director may release the levy as authorized under subparagraph (1) of this paragraph if he determines that the value of the interest of the United States in the seized property, or in the part of the seized property to be released, is insufficient to cover the expenses of the sale of such property."

Briefly looking at the different criteria for release, you should see that each one is available only at the discretion of the IRS. Your best strategy, therefore, is to be cooperative. The best approach was already lost if you are at the point of seizure.

However, not all collection agents are unreasonable. Demonstrate good faith and you can often get the seizure released. What is important is the demonstration of good faith. They have your property; now you must play by their rules. If you can show that but for the seizure you could get a loan to satisfy the tax liability or at least a substantial portion of it, there is an excellent chance you will be able to get the property released.

Do not believe that just because it seized your property, the IRS will go no further. The IRS will sell your property without hesitation if you do not act promptly to convince it to work with you. Recently, for example, the IRS went after singer Willie Nelson and sold his property to satisfy a large tax liability.

MOST IMPORTANTLY, do not let notices from the IRS go without attention or a response. If you are to the point of seizure, you are likely past the time to compromise or reduce the tax liability.

Can You Negotiate Your Tax Liability?

Often it is possible to reduce your payment of taxes to less than what you actually owe. The IRS has a procedure known as Offer and Compromise. The procedure follows Section 5712 of the IRS Tax Collection Guidelines.

The IRS will not approach you for offer and compromise. Quite simply, they will not volunteer to "bid against" themselves, but they will entertain such an offer.

As in the case of bankruptcy (see Chapter 5), the IRS will determine what your equity is and will require you to offer at least what they would receive had they levied or seized your property. The IRS is not required to accept offers in compromise, so your good faith is a prerequisite. For example, a client of mine was advised by his accountant to make an offer of $1.00. This was determined by the Collection Officer and his manager to be a bad faith offer. Thereafter, it took approximately five years to rehabilitate his credibility in order to satisfy his tax liability. Ultimately, he was unable to reduce his liability, although some penalties were reduced.

Form **433**
(Rev. Feb. 1982)

Department of the Treasury — Internal Revenue Service

Statement of Financial Condition and Other Information

(Please file in duplicate with offer in compromise)

Please furnish the information requested in this form with your offer in compromise, if the offer is based in whole or in part on inability to pay the liability. If you need help in preparing this statement, call on any Internal Revenue office. It is important that you answer all questions. If a question does not apply, please enter N/A. This will speed up consideration of your offer.

1a. Name(s) of Taxpayer(s)	b. Social Security Number	c. Employer Identification Number

d. Business Address	e. Bus. Tel. No.	2. Name and Address of Representative, if any
f. Home Address	g. Home Tel. No.	

3.	Kind of tax involved	Taxable period	Amount due	Amount offered
a.				
b.				
c.				
d.				
e.				

4.   Due and unpaid Federal taxes, *(except those covered by this offer in compromise)*

	Kind of tax	Taxable period	Amount due
a.			
b.			
c.			

5.   Names of banks and other financial institutions you have done business with at any time during past 3 years—

	Name and address		Name and address
a.		b.	
c.		d.	

e.   Do you rent a safety deposit box in your name or in any other name?

☐ No   ☐ Yes *(If yes, give name and address of bank)*

6.   If income withholding or employment tax is involved, please complete 6a through f

a.   Were the employees' income withholding or employment taxes, due from employees on wages they received from employment, deducted or withheld from the wages paid during any period shown above?   ☐ Yes   ☐ No

b.   If so, was the tax paid or deposited to the Internal Revenue Service?
☐ No   ☐ Yes

c.   If deducted but not paid or deposited to IRS, how did you dispose of the deducted amounts?

d.   Has business in which you incurred such taxes been discontinued?
☐ No   ☐ Yes

e.   If so, on what date was it discontinued?

f.   How did you dispose of assets of discontinued business?

7.   Offer filed by individual

a. Name of Spouse	b. Age of Spouse	c. Age of Taxpayer

d.	Names of dependent children or relatives	Relationship	Age
(1)			
(2)			
(3)			
(4)			
(5)			
(6)			
(7)			

Form 433 (Rev. 2-82)

Please furnish your most recent financial information. In the columns below, show the cost and fair market value of each asset you own directly or indirectly. Also show all your interests in estates, trusts, and other property rights, including contingent interests and remainders.

8. Statement of assets and liabilities as of _____ *(date)*

a.	Assets	Cost*	Fair market value
(1)	Cash	$	
(2)	Cash surrender value of insurance *(See item 9)*		
(3)	Accounts receivable *(See item 11)*		
(4)	Notes receivable *(See item 11)*		
(5)	Merchandise inventory *(See item 12)*		
(6)	Real estate *(See item 13)*		
(7)	Furniture and fixtures *(See item 14)*		
(8)	Machinery and equipment *(See item 14)*		
(9)	Trucks and delivery equipment *(See item 15)*		
(10)	Automobiles *(See item 15)*		
(11)	Securities *(See item 16)*		
(12)			
(13)			
(14)			
(15)			
(16)			
(17)			
(18)			
(19)			
(20)			
(21)			
(22)			
(23)			
(24)			
(25)			
(26)			
(27)	**Total assets** ▶	$	$

b.	Liabilities	Amount	
(1)	Loans on insurance *(See items 9 and 10)*	$	
(2)	Accounts payable		
(3)	Notes payable		
(4)	Mortgages *(See item 13)*		
(5)	Accrued real estate taxes *(See item 13)*		
(6)	Judgments *(See item 17)*		
(7)	Reserves *(Itemize)*		
(8)			
(9)			
(10)			
(11)			
(12)			
(13)			
(14)			
(15)			
(16)			
(17)			
(18)			
(19)			
(20)			
(21)			
(22)	**Total liabilities** ▶	$	

(*Less depreciation, if any)   Page 2   Form **433** (Rev. 2-82)

9.   Life insurance policies now in force with right to change beneficiary reserved

Number of Policy	Name of Company	Amount of Policy	Present Cash Surrender Value Plus Accumulated Dividends	Policy Loan	Date Made	Automatic Premium Payments*	Date Made
a.		$	$	$		$	
b.							
c.							
d.							
e.							
f.							
g.							
h.							
i.							
j.							

Show only those made before date notice of levy was served on the insurance company.

10.   Life insurance policies assigned or pledged on indebtedness

If any of the policies listed in item 9 are assigned or pledged on indebtedness, except with insurance companies, give the following information about each policy:

Number of Policy Assigned or Pledged	Name and Address of Pledgee or Assignee	Amount of Indebtedness	Date Pledged or Assigned
a.		$	
b.			
c.			
d.			
e.			
f.			
g.			

11.   Accounts and notes receivable

Name	Book Value	Liquidation Value	Amount of Indebtedness if Pledged	Date Pledged
a. Accounts Receivable				
(1)	$	$	$	
(2)				
(3)				
(4)				
(5)				
(6)				
(7)				
(8)				
(9)				
(10)				
(11)				
(12) Total ▶	$	$	$	
b. Notes Receivable				
(1)	$	$	$	
(2)				
(3)				
(4)				
(5)				
(6)				
(7)				
(8)				
(9)				
(10)				
(11) Total ▶	$	$	$	

     Form **433** (Rev. 2-82)

12.   Merchandise inventory

Description	Cost	Fair Market Value	Liquidation Value	Amount of Indebtedness If Pledged	Date Pledged
a. Raw material	$	$	$	$	
b. Work in progress					
c. Finished goods					
d. Supplies					
e. Other (Specify)					
f. Total ▶	$	$	$	$	

13.   Real estate

Description	Cost*	Fair Market Value	Balance Due on Mortgage	Date Mortgage Recorded	Unpaid Interest and Taxes
a.	$	$	$		$
b.					
c.					
d.					
e.					
f.					
g.					
h.					
i. Total ▶	$	$	$		$

14.   Furniture and fixtures — Machinery and equipment

Description	Cost*	Liquidation Value	Amount of Indebtedness If Pledged	Date Pledged
a. Furniture and fixtures (Business)	$	$	$	
b. Furniture (Household-residence)				
c. Machinery (Specify kind)				
d.				
e.				
f.				
g. Equipment (Except trucks and automobiles) (Specify)				
h.				
i.				
j.				
k. Total ▶	$	$	$	

15.   Trucks and automobiles

	Cost*	Liquidation Value	Amount of Indebtedness If Pledged	Date Pledged
a. Trucks	$	$	$	
b.				
c.				
d.				
e.				
f.				
g. Automobiles (Personal or used in business)				
h.				
i.				
j.				
k.				
l.				
m. Total ▶	$	$	$	

(*Less depreciation, if any)   Page 4   Form 433 (Rev. 2-82)

16. Securities (Bonds, stocks, etc.)

Name of company	Number of Units	Cost	Fair Market Value	Amount of Indebtedness If Pledged	Date Pledged
a.		$	$	$	
b.					
c.					
d.					
e.					
f.					
g.					
h.					
i. Total ▶		$	$	$	

17. Judgments

Name of Creditor	Amount of Judgment	Date Recorded	Where Recorded
a.	$		
b.			
c.			
d.			
e. Total ▶	$		

18. Statement of income — Corporation

IMPORTANT: If the offer in compromise is from a corporation, please furnish the information requested below *(from income tax returns, as adjusted, for past 2 years and from records for current year from January 1 to date).*

	19	19	Jan. 1 to 19
a. Gross income			
(1) Gross sales or receipts *(Subtract returns and allowances)*	$	$	$
(2) Cost of goods sold			
(3) Gross profit - trading or manufacturing			
(4) Gross profit - from other sources			
(5) Interest income			
(6) Rents and royalties			
(7) Gains and losses *(From Schedule D)*			
(8) Dividends			
(9) Other *(Specify)*			
(10) Total income ▶	$	$	$
b. Deductions			
(1) Compensation of officers	$	$	$
(2) Salaries and wages *(Not deducted elsewhere)*			
(3) Rents			
(4) Repairs			
(5) Bad Debts			
(6) Interest			
(7) Taxes			
(8) Losses			
(9) Dividends			
(10) Depreciation and depletion			
(11) Contributions			
(12) Advertising			
(13) Other *(Specify)*			
(14)			
(15) Total deductions ▶	$	$	$
c. Net income *(loss)* ▶	$	$	$
d. Nontaxable income ▶	$	$	$
e. Unallowable deductions ▶	$	$	$

Form **433** (Rev. 2-82)

19. Salaries paid to principal officers and dividends distributed — Corporation

IMPORTANT: If the offer in compromise is from a corporation, please show salaries paid to principal officers for past 3 years and amounts distributed in dividends, if any, during and since the taxable years covered by this offer.

a. Salaries paid to (Name and Title)		19	19	19
(1)	, President	$	$	$
(2)	, Vice President			
(3)	, Treasurer			
(4)	, Secretary			
(5)				
(6)				
(7) Total ►		$	$	$

b.	Year	Dividends Paid		Year	Dividends Paid		Year	Dividends Paid
(1)		$	(8)		$	(15)		$
(2)	.		(9)			(16)		
(3)			(10)			(17)		
(4)			(11)			(18)		
(5)			(12)			(19)		
(6)			(13)					
(7)		$	(14)		$	(20)	Total	$

20. Statement of income — Individual

IMPORTANT: If the offer in compromise is from an individual or an estate, please furnish information requested below *(from income tax returns as adjusted for past 2 years)*.

a. Gross income		19	19
(1)	Salaries, wages, commissions	$	$
(2)	Dividends		
(3)	Interest		
(4)	Income from business or profession		
(5)	Partnership income		
(6)	Gains or losses *(From Schedule D, Form 1040)*		
(7)	Annuities and pensions		
(8)	Rents and royalties		
(9)	Income from estates and trusts		
(10)			
(11)			
(12)			
(13)			
(14)			
(15)	Total income ►	$	$

b. Deductions		19	19
(1)	Contributions	$	$
(2)	Interest paid		
(3)	Taxes paid		
(4)	Casualty losses *(by fire, storm, etc.)*		
(5)	Medical expenses		
(6)	Bad debts		
(7)			
(8)			
(9)			
(10)			
(11)			
(12)	Total deductions ►	$	$

c. Net income (loss) ►	$	$
d. Nontaxable income ►	$	$
e. Unallowable deductions ►	$	$

Form **433** (Rev. 2-82)

21.	Receipts and disbursements — Individual	From	To

If the offer in compromise is from an individual or on behalf of an estate, please furnish below a complete analysis of receipts and disbursements for the past 12 months.

a. Receipts

Description	Source From Which Received	Amount
(1) Salary		$
(2) Commissions		
(3) Business or profession		
(4) Dividends		
(5) Interest		
(6) Annuities or pensions		
(7) Rents and royalties		
(8) Sale of assets (Net amount received)		
(9) Amounts borrowed		
(10) Gifts		
(11)		
(12)		
(13)		
(14)		
(15)		
(16)		
(17)		
(18)		
Total receipts ▶		$

b. Disbursements

Description	Amount
(1) Debt reduction	$
(2) Interest	
(3) Federal taxes	
(4) Other taxes	
(5) Insurance premiums	
(6) Medical expenses	
(7) Automobile expenses	
(8) Servant's wages	
(9) Gifts	
(10) Living expenses (Itemize)	
Total disbursements ▶	$

Form **433** (Rev. 2-82)

22. Disposal of assets—From the beginning of the taxable period covered by this offer in compromise to the present date, have you disposed of any assets or property with a cost or fair market value of more than $500, except for full value at the time of sale, transfer, exchange, gift or other disposition?

☐ No   ☐ Yes *(If yes, please furnish the following information)*

Description of Asset	Date of Transfer	Fair Market Value When Transferred	Consideration Received	Relationship of Transferee to Taxpayer
		$	$	

23. Interest in or beneficiary of estate or trust — Have you any life interest or remainder interest, either vested or contingent in any trust or estate, or are you a beneficiary of any trust?

☐ No   ☐ Yes *(If yes, please furnish a copy of the instrument creating the trust or estate — Also give the following information)*

Name of Trust or Estate	Present Value of Assets	Value of Your Interest	Annual Income Received From This Source
	$	$	$

24. Grantor, donor, trustee or fiduciary — Are you the grantor or donor of any trust, or the trustee or fiduciary for any trust?

☐ No   ☐ Yes *(If yes, please furnish a copy of the instrument creating the trust. Also give present value of corpus of trust, and any other pertinent information.)*

25. Any other assets or interests in assets — Have you any other assets or an interest in assets either actual or contingent, other than those listed here *(i.e., Profit-sharing plan or pension plan)*?

☐ No   ☐ Yes *(If yes, please describe the assets)*

26a. Are foreclosure proceedings pending on any real estate which you own or have an interest in? ☐ No ☐ Yes	b. If yes, please give location of real estate.	c. Was the government made a party to the suit? ☐ No ☐ Yes
27a. Are bankruptcy or receivership proceedings pending? ☐ No ☐ Yes		b. If a corporation, is it in process of liquidation? ☐ No ☐ Yes

28. Is the sum offered in compromise borrowed money? *(If yes, please give name and address of lender and list collateral, if any, pledged to secure the loan.)*

☐ No   ☐ Yes

29. What is the prospect of an increase in value of assets or in present income? *(Please give general statement)*

30.   **Affidavit**

Under penalties of perjury, I declare that I have examined the information given in this statement and, to the best of my knowledge and belief, it is true, correct, and complete, and I further declare that I have no assets, owned either directly or indirectly, or income of any nature other than as shown in this statement.

a. Date of this statement	b. Signature

Form **433** (Rev. 2-82)

How to prepare a Collection Information Statement

Complete all blocks, except shaded areas. Write "N/A" (Not Applicable) in those blocks that do not apply to you. *If the form is not completed, we will not be able to assist you in determining the best method for you to pay the amount due.* The areas explained below are those which we have found to be the most confusing to those completing the form.

Section III

Item 21—Bank Accounts

Enter all accounts even if there is currently no balance. *Do Not* enter bank loans.

Item 22—Bank Charge Cards, Lines of Credit, etc.

Enter only credit issued by a bank, credit union, or savings and loan (MasterCard, Visa, overdraft protection, etc.). List other charge accounts such as oil companies and department stores in Item 35.

Item 24—Real Property Description and Ownership

List all real estate that you own or are purchasing. Include the address, county, and type of buildings on the property. List the names of all owners and type of ownership (such as joint tenants, tenant in common, etc.).

Item 25—Life Insurance

Under the heading "type," indicate if it is whole life or term life.

Section IV

Items 31 thru 33—Vehicles, Real Property, and Other Assets

Current Market Value - Indicate the amount you could sell the asset for today.

Liabilities Balance Due - Enter the current amount owed on the loan, mortgage, etc.

Equity in Asset - Subtract liability from current market value.

Date Pledged - Enter the date the loan was originally taken out.

Date of Final Payment - Enter the date the loan will be fully paid. If you are behind in payments, enter "Behind."

List other assets you own such as campers, boats, jewelry, antiques, etc. in item 33.

Item 35—Other Liabilities

List all other liabilities, including charge accounts, bank loans and notes, personal loans, medical bills, etc.

Section V

If only one spouse has a tax liability, but both have income, the total household income and expenses should be listed.

Items 38 and 39—Wages/Salaries

To determine net salary, deduct only mandatory items from your gross salary, such as social security and other withheld taxes, and company retirement. Do not deduct allotments you elect to take out of the check such as insurance payments, credit union deductions, car payments, etc. List these as expenses in **Section IV** or **Section V**.

Item 41—Net Business Income

If you are self employed, enter your monthly *Net* business income, that is, what you earn after you have paid your ordinary and necessary monthly business expenses.

Necessary Living Expenses

Expenses must be reasonable for the size of your family, geographic location and unique circumstances.

Item 49—Rent

Enter your monthly rent payment. If you are a homeowner, write N/A.

Item 51—Allowable Installment Payments

Do not show any entry in this space. IRS use only.

Item 52—Utilities

Show the total utility expenses in the amount column. List the amount for each utility separately in the space beside that utility. If you need additional space, use Remarks area or a separate sheet of paper.

Item 53—Transportation

Enter the average monthly expense for gasoline, oil, parking, or public transportation.

Item 54—Insurance

Show the total insurance expenses in the amount column. List the amount for each insurance separately such as life, health, homeowners, and auto in the space beside it. If you need additional space, attach a separate sheet of paper.

Item 55—Medical

Show recurring medical expenses only. Do not include an occasional medical expense.

Item 56—Estimated Tax Payments

Enter the monthly average you pay on your estimated tax. Send a copy of your most recent canceled check or money order receipt as proof of payment.

Items 59 and 60—Total and Net Difference

Do not show an entry in these spaces. IRS use only.

Certification

For joint income tax liabilities, both husband and wife should sign the statement.

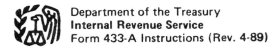 Department of the Treasury
Internal Revenue Service
Form 433-A Instructions (Rev. 4-89)

Form 433-A
(Rev. April 1989)

Department of the Treasury — Internal Revenue Service

Collection Information Statement for Individuals

NOTE: Complete all blocks, except shaded areas. Write "N/A" *(not applicable)* **in those blocks that do not apply.**

1. Taxpayers' names and address *(including County)*	2. Home phone number ( )	3. Marital status
County _____	4. Social Security Numbers	a. Taxpayer	b. Spouse

Section I.   Employment Information

5. Taxpayer's employer or business *(name and address)*	5a. How long employed	6. Business phone number ( )	7. Occupation
	5b. Number of exemptions claimed on Form W-4	8. Paydays	9. *(Check appropriate box)* ☐ Wage earner ☐ Partner ☐ Sole proprietor
10. Spouse's employer or business *(name and address)*	10a. How long employed	11. Business phone number ( )	12. Occupation
	10b. Number of exemptions claimed on Form W-4	13. Paydays	14. *(Check appropriate box)* ☐ Wage earner ☐ Partner ☐ Sole proprietor

Section II.   Personal Information

15. Name, address and telephone number of next of kin or other reference

16. Age and relationship of dependents *(exclude yourself and spouse)* living in your household

17. Date of birth ▶	a. Taxpayer	b. Spouse	

Section III.   General Financial Information

18. Latest filed income tax return *(tax year)*	19. Number of exemptions claimed	20. Adjusted Gross Income	

21. Bank accounts *(Include Savings & Loans, Credit Unions, IRA and Retirement Plans, Certificates of Deposit, etc.)*

Name of Institution	Address	Type of Account	Account No.	Balance
Total *(Enter in Item 28)*			▶	

Section III — continued	General Financial Information

22. Bank charge cards, Credit Unions, Savings and Loans, Lines of credit

Type of Account or Card	Name and Address of Financial Institution	Monthly Payment	Credit Limit	Amount Owed	Credit Available
Totals *(Enter in Item 34)*	▶				

23. Safe deposit boxes rented or accessed *(List all locations, box numbers, and contents)*

24.	**Real Property** *(Brief description and type of ownership)*	**Physical Address**
a.		County _____
b.		County _____
c.		County _____

25.	**Life Insurance** *(Name of Company)*	Policy Number	Type	Face Amount	Available Loan Value
Total *(Enter in Item 30)*			▶	

26. Other information relating to your financial condition. If you check the yes box, please give dates and explain under remarks.

a. Court proceedings	☐ Yes ☐ No	b. Bankruptcies	☐ Yes ☐ No
c. Repossessions	☐ Yes ☐ No	d. Recent transfer of assets for less than full value	☐ Yes ☐ No
e. Anticipated increase in income	☐ Yes ☐ No	f. Participant or beneficiary to trust, estate, profit sharing, etc.	☐ Yes ☐ No

Remarks

Section IV.   Asset and Liability Analysis

Description	Current Market Value	Liabilities Balance Due	Equity in Asset	Amount of Monthly Payment	Name and Address of Lien/Note Holder/Obligee	Date Pledged	Date of Final Payment
7. Cash							
8. Bank accounts *(from Item 21)*							
9. Stocks, Bonds, Investments							
0. Cash or loan value of Insur.							
1. Vehicles *(Model, year, license, tag #)*							
a.							
b.							
c.							
2. Real property *(From Section III, item 24)* a. / b. / c.							
3. Other assets							
a.							
b.							
c.							
d.							
e.							
4. Bank revolving credit *(from Item 22)*							
5. Other Liabilities *(Include judgments, notes, and other charge accounts)* a.							
b.							
c.							
d.							
e.							
f.							
g.							
6. Federal taxes owed							
7. Totals			$	$			

Internal Revenue Service Use Only Below This Line

Financial Verification/Analysis

Item	Date Information or Encumbrance Verified	Date Property Inspected	Estimated Forced Sale Equity
Personal Residence			
Other Real Property			
Vehicles			
Other Personal Property			
State Employment *(Husband and Wife)*			
Income Tax Return			
Wage Statements *(Husband and Wife)*			
Sources of Income/Credit *(D&B Report)*			
Expenses			
Other Assets/Liabilities			

Form **433-A**   page 3   (Rev. 4-89)

Section V.   Monthly Income and Expense Analysis

Income			Necessary Living Expenses	
Source	**Gross**	**Net**		
38. Wages/Salaries *(Taxpayer)*	$	$	49. Rent (Do not show mortgage listed in item 32)	$
39. Wages/Salaries *(Spouse)*			50. Groceries (no. of people _____)	
40. Interest - Dividends			51. Allowable installment payments *(IRS use only)*	
41. Net business income *(from Form 433-B)*			52. Utilities (Gas $_____ Water $_____	
42. Rental income			Electric $_____ Phone $_____)	
43. Pension *(Taxpayer)*			53. Transportation	
44. Pension *(Spouse)*			54. Insurance (Life $_____ Health $_____	
45. Child Support			Home $_____ Car $_____)	
46. Alimony			55. Medical *(Expenses not covered in item 54)*	
47. Other			56. Estimated tax payments	
			57. Court ordered payments	
			58. Other expenses (specify)	
48. **Total**	$	$	59. **Total** *(IRS use only)*	$
			60. Net difference *(income less necessary living expenses)* *(IRS use only)*	$

Certification   **Under penalties of perjury, I declare that to the best of my knowledge and belief this statement of assets, liabilities, and other information is true, correct, and complete.**

61. Your signature	62. Spouse's signature *(if joint return was filed)*	63. Date

Internal Revenue Service Use Only Below This Line

Explain any difference between Item 60 and installment agreement amount:

Additional information or comments:

Name of Originator and IDRS assignment number	Date

Form **433-A**   page 4   (Rev. 4-89)

Form **433-B**
(Rev. April 1989)

Department of the Treasury — Internal Revenue Service

Collection Information Statement for Businesses

(If you need additional space, please attach a separate sheet)

1. Name and address of business	2. Business phone number ( )
	3. *(Check appropriate box)*

3. *(Check appropriate box)*
- [ ] Sole proprietor
- [ ] Partnership
- [ ] Corporation
- [ ] Other *(specify)*

County_____

4. Name and title of person being interviewed	5. Employer Identification Number	6. Type of business

7. Information about owner, partners, officers, major shareholder, etc.

Name and Title	Effective Date	Home Address	Phone Number	Social Security Number	Total Shares or Interest

Section I. General Financial Information

8. Latest filed income tax return ▶	Form	Tax Year ended	Net income before taxes

9. Bank accounts *(List all types of accounts including payroll and general, savings, certificates of deposit, etc.)*

Name of Institution	Address	Type of Account	Account Number	Balance
		Total *(Enter in Item 17)* ▶		

10. Bank credit available *(Lines of credit, etc.)*

Name of Institution	Address	Credit Limit	Amount Owed	Credit Available	Monthly Payments
Totals *(Enter in Items 24 or 25 as appropriate)* ▶					

11. Location, box number, and contents of all safe deposit boxes rented or accessed

Section I — *continued*   General Financial Information

12. Real property

Brief Description and Type of Ownership	Physical Address
a.	County _____
b.	County _____
c.	County _____
d.	County _____

13. Life insurance policies owned with business as beneficiary

Name Insured	Company	Policy Number	Type	Face Amount	Available Loan Value
		Total *(Enter in Item 19)*		▶	

14. Additional information regarding financial condition *(Court proceedings, bankruptcies filed or anticipated, transfers of assets for less than full value, changes in market conditions, etc.; include information regarding company participation in trusts, estates, profit-sharing plans, etc.)*

15. Accounts/Notes receivable *(Include current contract jobs, loans to stockholders, officers, partners, etc.)*

Name	Address	Amount Due	Date Due	Status
		$		
	Total *(Enter in Item 18)* ▶	$		

Form **433-B** (Rev. 4-89)

Section II.

Asset and Liability Analysis

Description (a)	Cur. Mkt. Value (b)	Liabilities Bal. Due (c)	Equity in Asset (d)	Amt. of Mo. Pymt. (e)	Name and Address of Lien/Note Holder/Obligee (f)	Date Pledged (g)	Date of Final Pymt. (h)
16. Cash on hand							
17. Bank accounts							
18. Accounts/Notes receivable							
19. Life insurance loan value							
20. Real property (from Item 12) a.							
b.							
c.							
d.							
21. Vehicles (Model, year, and license) a.							
b.							
c.							
22. Machinery and equipment (Specify) a.							
b.							
c.							
23. Merchandise inventory (Specify) a.							
b.							
24. Other assets (Specify) a.							
b.							
25. Other liabilities (Include notes and judgments) a.							
b.							
c.							
d.							
e.							
f.							
g.							
h.							
26. Federal taxes owed							
27. Total							

Form **433-B** (Rev. 4-89)

Section III.   Income and Expense Analysis

The following information applies to income and expenses during the period _____ to _____		Accounting method used	
Income		**Expenses**	
28. Gross receipts from sales, services, etc.	$	34. Materials purchased	$
29. Gross rental income		35. Net wages and salaries Number of Employees _____	
30. Interest		36. Rent	
31. Dividends		37. Allowable installment payments *(IRS use only)*	
32. Other income *(Specify)*		38. Supplies	
		39. Utilities/Telephone	
		40. Gasoline/Oil	
		41. Repairs and maintenance	
		42. Insurance	
		43. Current taxes	
		44. Other *(Specify)*	
33. Total ▶	$	45. Total *(IRS use only)* ▶	$
		46. **Net difference** *(IRS use only)* ▶	$

Certification Under penalties of perjury, I declare that to the best of my knowledge and belief this statement of assets, liabilities, and other information is true, correct, and complete.

47. Signature	48. Date

Internal Revenue Service Use Only Below This Line

Financial Verification/Analysis

Item	Date Information or Encumbrance Verified	Date Property Inspected	Estimated Forced Sale Equity
Sources of Income/Credit (D&B Report)			
Expenses			
Real Property			
Vehicles			
Machinery and Equipment			
Merchandise			
Accounts/Notes Receivable			
Corporate Information, if Applicable			
U.C.C. : Senior/Junior Lienholder			
Other Assets/Liabilities:			

Explain difference between Item 46 (or P&L) and installment agreement amount: (If Form 433-A is not used)

Name of Originator and IDRS assignment number	Date

306 10-89

Form **433-D**
(Rev. April 1989)

Department of the Treasury — Internal Revenue Service

Installment Agreement

Name and address of taxpayer(s)	Social security or employer identification number	Agreement locator number
	Kinds of taxes *(Form numbers)*	
	Tax periods	Agreement review date
	Amount of tax owed	

The undersigned agrees that the Federal taxes shown above, plus any interest and penalties provided by law, will be paid as follows:

$_____ to be paid on _____ and $ _____ to be paid

on the _____ of each _____ thereafter until the liability is paid in full, and also agrees that the above tax

installments will be increased or decreased as follows:

Date of increase (or decrease)					
Amount of change	$				
New installment amount	$				

Conditions:

- This agreement is based on your current financial circumstances and is subject to revision or termination if subsequent financial information required by IRS reflects a change in your ability to pay.
- Failure to provide updated financial information when requested by the Service will be reason for termination of this agreement.
- All Federal taxes that become due during the term of this agreement must be paid on time.
- All Federal tax returns that become due during the term of this agreement must be filed on time.
- Any Federal or State refunds that might otherwise be due will be applied to this liability until it is satisfied.
- If the Conditions of this Installment Agreement are not met, it will be terminated and the entire tax liability may be collected by levy on income, bank accounts, or any other assets, or by seizure of property.
- This agreement may be terminated if collection of the tax liability is endangered.
- **This agreement may require managerial approval; you will be notified if it is not approved.**

Additional conditions:	Originator's name, title and IDRS assignment number:

Your signature	Title *(if corporate officer or partner)*	Date	For assistance call:
Spouse's signature *(if joint liability)*		Date	or write:
Agreement examined or approved by *(signature, title, function)*		Date	

General Information

Employer *(Name and address)*	Taxpayer's Telephone Number(s) ▶	*(Home)*
		(Business)

Banks *(Names and addresses)*

Notice of Federal tax lien filing determination *(check one)*		Earliest CSED
☐ Notice of tax lien not required	☐ Notice of tax lien filed	
☐ Notice of tax lien not filed *(Form 3991 attached)*	☐ Notice of tax lien to be filed County/State _____ taxpayer notified	

Form **433-D** (Rev. 4-89)

321 7-90

Form 433-F
(Rev. May 1990)

Department of the Treasury - Internal Revenue Service

Collection Information Statement

(If you need additional space, please attach a separate sheet with your name(s) and Social Security number(s).)

Your name(s) and address (Including county)	Phone numbers (circle best daytime number)
	Home:
	Your work:
	Your spouse's work:
	Social Security numbers
	Yours: Your Spouse's
Your employer or business (name and address)	Your spouse's employer or business (name and address)

Real estate *(Home and other Real Estate)*

County/Description	Value	Balance Owed	Equity	Monthly Payment

Other assets *(Cars, Boats, RV's, etc.)*

County/Description	Value	Balance Owed	Equity	Monthly Payment

Bank accounts *(include Savings & Loans, Credit Unions, Certificates of Deposit, Individual Retirement Accounts, Lines of Credit, etc.)*

Name of Institution	Address	Type of account	Balance

Monthly Income

Your net pay	$
Your spouse's net pay	
Social Security or Pensions	
Profit from your business	
Other income (source):	
Total income	$

Monthly Expenses

Rent	$
Groceries	
Utilities (Electricity, Heating, Gas, Water, Phone)	
Transportation (gas, bus fares)	
Medical (doctors, & medicine not paid by insurance)	
Insurance (Auto, Health, Life, Homeowners/Rental)	
Estimated Tax Payment (1040ES)	
Other (explain)	
Credit Cards	
Loan Payments (not listed above)	

Additional Information *(expected changes to income, health, etc.)*

Under penalties of perjury, I declare that to the best of my knowledge and belief this statement of assets, liabilities, and other information is true, correct, and complete.

Your signature	Spouse's signature	Date

Catalog No. 62053Y   [The next page is 1061-7.]   Form **433-F** (Rev. 5-90)

Form **433-D**
(Rev. April 1989)

Department of the Treasury – Internal Revenue Service
Installment Agreement

Name and address of taxpayer(s)	Social security or employer identification number	Agreement locator number
	Kinds of taxes *(Form numbers)*	_____
	Tax periods	Agreement review date
	Amount of tax owed	_____

The undersigned agrees that the Federal taxes shown above, plus any interest and penalties provided by law, will be paid as follows:

$_____ to be paid on _____ and $_____ to be paid

on the _____ of each _____ thereafter until the liability is paid in full, and also agrees that the above tax

installments will be increased or decreased as follows:

Date of increase (or decrease)					
Amount of change	$				
New installment amount	$				

Conditions:

- This agreement is based on your current financial circumstances and is subject to revision or termination if subsequent financial information required by IRS reflects a change in your ability to pay.
- Failure to provide updated financial information when requested by the Service will be reason for termination of this agreement.
- All Federal taxes that become due during the term of this agreement must be paid on time.
- All Federal tax returns that become due during the term of this agreement must be filed on time.
- Any Federal or State refunds that might otherwise be due will be applied to this liability until it is satisfied.
- If the Conditions of this Installment Agreement are not met, it will be terminated and the entire tax liability may be collected by levy on income, bank accounts, or any other assets, or by seizure of property.
- This agreement may be terminated if collection of the tax liability is endangered.
- **This agreement may require managerial approval; you will be notified if it is not approved.**

Additional conditions:	Originator's name, title and IDRS assignment number:

Your signature	Title *(if corporate officer or partner)*	Date	For assistance call:
Spouse's signature *(if joint liability)*		Date	or write:
Agreement examined or approved by *(signature, title, function)*		Date	

General Information

Employer *(Name and address)*	Taxpayer's Telephone Number(s) ▶	*(Home)*
		(Business)

Banks *(Names and addresses)*

Notice of Federal tax lien filing determination *(check one)*

		Earliest CSED
☐ Notice of tax lien not required	☐ Notice of tax lien filed	
☐ Notice of tax lien not filed *(Form 3991 attached)*	☐ Notice of tax lien to be filed County/State _____ taxpayer notified	

Part 1 – IRS Office Copy Form **433-D** (Rev. 4-89)

321 7-90

Form **433-F**
(Rev. May 1990)

Department of the Treasury - Internal Revenue Service

Collection Information Statement

(If you need additional space, please attach a separate sheet with your name(s) and Social Security number(s).

Your name(s) and address (Including county)	Phone numbers (circle best daytime number)
	Home:
	Your work:
	Your spouse's work:
	Social Security numbers
	Yours: Your Spouse's
Your employer or business (name and address)	Your spouse's employer or business (name and address)

Real estate *(Home and other Real Estate)*

County/Description	Value	Balance Owed	Equity	Monthly Payment

Other assets *(Cars, Boats, RV's, etc.)*

County/Description	Value	Balance Owed	Equity	Monthly Payment

Bank accounts *(include Savings & Loans, Credit Unions, Certificates of Deposit, Individual Retirement Accounts, Lines of Credit, etc.)*

Name of Institution	Address	Type of account	Balance

Monthly Income

Your net pay	$
Your spouse's net pay	
Social Security or Pensions	
Profit from your business	
Other income (source):	
Total income	$

Monthly Expenses

Rent	$
Groceries	
Utilities (Electricity, Heating, Gas, Water, Phone)	
Transportation (gas, bus fares)	
Medical (doctors, & medicine not paid by insurance)	
Insurance (Auto, Health, Life, Homeowners/Rental)	
Estimated Tax Payment (1040ES)	
Other (explain)	
Credit Cards	
Loan Payments (not listed above)	

Additional Information *(expected changes to income, health, etc.)*

Under penalties of perjury, I declare that to the best of my knowledge and belief this statement of assets, liabilities, and other information is true, correct, and complete.

Your signature	Spouse's signature	Date

Catalog No. 62053Y   [The next page is 1061-7.]   Form **433-F** (Rev. 5-90)

Form 433-G
(Rev. February 1990)

Department of the Treasury — Internal Revenue Service
Direct Debit Installment Agreement

Instructions

Fill out the identifying information on the top part of the form.

Enter your name, address, and social security number or employer identification number in the blanks provided.

Fill in the block for Kinds of Taxes (Form numbers), Tax Periods, and Amount of tax owed if you know the information.

Next, read the section that begins "The undersigned agrees ..." In the first blank space, enter the amount you are paying with this agreement. If you were contacted by an IRS employee regarding this matter, you must pay the amount agreed upon during your interview.

In the second blank space, enter the amount of your monthly installment.

Using your calendar, enter in the last space, the date that is seven weeks from the date you are mailing this form back to us. This is the earliest date IRS will take money from your account electronically. If this date is the 29th, 30th, or 31st of the month, enter the 1st day of the following month as the due date. Remember to record this date and the payment amount in your checkbook.

On the same day of each month, until your liability is satisfied, your bank account will be debited for this agreement amount and forwarded to IRS. For example, if your first payment falls on May 20th, your account will be debited each month on the 20th. You must update your checkbook. You will receive no reminder notices from IRS.

Read the Conditions of Agreement and check the line indicating whether your account is used primarily for business or personal use.

Attach a blank, voided check for the bank account you will use for the agreement. We cannot process your agreement without this check.

Sign and date the agreement. We cannot accept an unsigned agreement.

Finally, fill in the Employer information, Bank information (financial institutions or accounts other than the one on the above check), and your Telephone Numbers.

Be sure to attach the bottom part of your notice or letter (if you received one) to the payment you send along with Parts 1 & 3 of your agreement.

Contact IRS at our toll free number if you have questions regarding the Direct Debit process or the completion of this form.

Taxpayer's Instructions   Form **433-G** (Rev. 2-90)

319 5-90

1061-7

Form **433-G**
(Rev. February 1990)

Department of the Treasury — Internal Revenue Service
Direct Debit Installment Agreement

Agreement Locator Number

Name and address of taxpayer(s)

County: _____

Social security or employer identification number

Kinds of taxes *(Form numbers)*

Tax periods

Amount of tax owed

The undersigned agrees that the Federal taxes shown above, plus any interest and penalties provided by law, will be paid as follows:

$_____ paid with this agreement, $_____ to be paid on _____ and on the same day of each month there-

after until the liability is paid in full and also agrees that the above tax installment payments will be increased or decreased as follows:

Date of increase/decrease			
Amount of increase/decrease			
New installment agreement amount			

Conditions of this agreement

- This agreement is based on your current financial circumstances and is subject to revision or termination if subsequent financial statements required by IRS reflect a change in your ability to pay.
- This agreement may require managerial approval. If it is not approved, you will be so notified.
- All Federal taxes that become due during the term of this agreement must be paid on time.
- All Federal tax returns that become due during the term of this agreement must be filed on time.
- Any Federal or State refunds that might otherwise be due will be applied to this liability until this liability is satisfied.
- This agreement to make installment payments may be terminated and the entire tax liability may be collected by levy on income, bank accounts, or other assets, or by seizure of property if the conditions of this agreement are not met, or if it is determined that collection of these taxes is in jeopardy.
- I (we) authorize the IRS and the Depository (bank) identified on the attached voided check to deduct payments (debit) from my (our) checking account or correct errors on the account. This authorization remains in effect until I (or either of us) notify IRS in writing to stop or until the liability covered by this agreement is satisfied.
- I (we) understand that if the DEPOSITORY is unable to honor IRS's request for payment due to insufficient funds in my (our) account on the payment due date I (we) will be charged a penalty of $15.00 or two percent of the payment request, whichever is greater. If the payment request is for less than $15.00, the penalty is the amount of the request.
- This account is used primarily for personal _____ business _____ transactions *(check one)*

Additional conditions

Originator's name, IDRS assignment number and function

┌ **Attach your blank, voided check here.**

For assistance call:

Or write:

Your signature	Title	Date
Spouse's signature *(if joint liability)*		Date
Agreement examined or approved by *(signature)*		Date

Taxpayer's telephone number:

(Home):

(Business):

Employer *(name & address)*

Banks *(name & address)* and account numbers

Part 1 - IRS Copy

Form **433-G** (Rev. 2-90)

IRS TAX COLLECTION GUIDELINES

COLLECTION ACTIVITY

5223

Analysis of Taxpayer's Financial Condition

(1)   The analysis of the taxpayer's financial condition provides the interviewer with a basis to make one or more of the following decisions:

    (a)   require payment from available assets;

    (b)   secure a short-term agreement or a longer installment agreement;

    (c)   report the account currently not collectible;

    (d)   recommend or initiate enforcement action (this would also be based on the results of the interview);

    (e)   file a Notice of Federal Tax Lien; and/or

    (f)   explain the offer in compromise provisions of the Code to the taxpayer.

(2)   In all steps that follow, information on the financial statement will be compared with other financial information provided by the taxpayer, particularly the copy of the taxpayer's latest Form 1040. If there are significant discrepancies, they should be discussed with the taxpayer. In the event further documentation is needed, it will be the taxpayer's responsibility to provide it. Discrepancies and their resolution will be noted in the case file history.

(3)   Analyze assets to determine ways of liquidating the account:

    (a)   if the taxpayer has cash equal to the tax liability, demand immediate payment;

    (b)   otherwise, review other assets which may be pledged or readily converted to cash (such as stocks and bonds, loan value of life insurance policies, etc.);

    (c)   if necessary, review any unencumbered assets, equity in encumbered assets, interests in estates and trusts, lines of credit (including available credit on bank charge cards), etc., from which money may be secured to make payment. In addition, consider the taxpayer's ability to make an unsecured loan. If the taxpayer belongs to a credit union, the taxpayer will be asked to borrow from that source. Upon identification of potential sources of loans, establish a date that the taxpayer is expected to make payments; and

    (d)   if there appears to be no borrowing ability, attempt to get the taxpayer to defer payment of other debts in order to pay the tax first.

(4) When analysis of the taxpayer's assets has given no obvious solution for liquidating the liability, the income and expenses should be analyzed.

    (a) When deciding what is an allowable expense item, the employee may allow:

        1. expenses which are necessary for the taxpayer's production of income (for example, dues for a trade union or professional organization; child care payments which allow a taxpayer to work);

        2. expenses which provide for the health and welfare of the taxpayer and family. The expense must be reasonable for the size of the family and the geographic location, as well as any unique individual circumstances. An expense will not be allowed if it serves to provide an elevated standard of living, as opposed to basic necessities. Also, an expense will not be allowed if the taxpayer has a proven record of not making the payment. Expenses allowable under this category are:

            a. rent or mortgage for place of residence;

            b. food;

            c. clothing;

            d. necessary transportation expense (auto insurance, car payment, bus fare, etc.);

            e. home maintenance expense (utilities, home-owner insurance, home-owner dues, etc.);

            f. medical expenses; health insurance;

            g. current tax payments (including federal, state and local);

            h. life insurance, but not if it is excessive to the point of being construed as an investment;

            i. alimony, child support or other court-ordered payment.

        3. Minimum payments on secured or legally perfected debts (car payments, judgments, etc.) will normally be allowed. However, if the encumbered asset represents an item which would not be considered a necessary living expense (e.g., a boat, recreational vehicle, etc.), the taxpayer should be advised that the debt payment will not be included as an allowable expense.

        4. Payments on unsecured debts (credit cards, personal loans, etc.) may not be allowed if omitting them would permit the taxpayer to pay in full within 90 days. However, if the taxpayer cannot fully pay within that time, minimum payments may be allowed if failure to make them would

ultimately impair the taxpayer's ability to pay the tax. The taxpayer should be advised that since all necessary living expenses have been allowed, no additional charge debts should be incurred. Generally, payments to friends or relatives will not be allowed. Dates for final payments on loans or installment purchases, as well as final payments on revolving credit arrangements after allowing minimum required payments, will be noted so the additional funds will be applied to the liability when they become available. If permitting the taxpayer to pay unsecured debts results in inability to pay or in only having a small amount left for payment of the tax, the taxpayer should be advised that a portion of the money available for payment of debts will be used for payment of the taxes and that arrangements must be made with other creditors accordingly.

(b)   As a general rule, expenses not specified in (a) above will be disallowed. However, an otherwise disallowable expense may be included if the employee believes an exception should be made based on the circumstances of the individual case. For instance, if the taxpayer advises that an educational expense or church contribution is a necessity, the individual circumstances must be considered. If an exception is made, document the case history to explain the basis for the exception.

(c)   The taxpayer will be required to verify and support any expense which appears excessive based on the income and circumstances of that taxpayer. However, proof of payment does not automatically make an item allowable. The criteria in (4)(a) apply.

(d)   In some cases, expense items or payments will not be due in even monthly increments. For instance, personal property tax may be due once a year. Unless the taxpayer substantiates that money is being set aside on a monthly basis, the expense will be allowed in total in the month due and the payment agreement adjusted accordingly for that month. Expense items with varying monthly payments should be averaged over a twelve-month period unless the variation will be excessive. In such instances, exclude the irregular months from the average. For example, if a utility bill will be excessive during the three winter months, average the other nine months.

(e)   In arriving at available net income, analyze the taxpayer's deductions to ensure that they are reasonable and allowable. The only automatically allowable deductions from gross pay or income are federal, state and local taxes (including FICA or other mandatory retirement program).

1. Other deductions from gross pay or income will be treated and listed as expenses, but only to the extent they meet the criteria in (4)(a) above.

2. To avoid affording the taxpayer a double deduction for one expense, ensure that such amounts remain in the total net pay figure and are also entered on the expense side of the income and expense analysis.

3. If the exemptions on the W-4 are going to be decreased, make the appropriate adjustments in the net income figures.

(f) To reach an average monthly take-home pay for taxpayers paid on a weekly basis, multiply the weekly pay times 52 weeks divided by 12 months (or multiply amount times 4.3 weeks). If the taxpayer is paid biweekly, multiply pay times 26 weeks divided by 12 months (or multiply amount times $2\,1/6$). If the taxpayer is paid semimonthly, multiply pay times 2.

(g) The amount to be paid monthly on an installment agreement payment will be at least the difference between the taxpayer's net income and allowable expenses. If the taxpayer will not consent to the proposed installment agreement, he/she should be advised that enforced collection action may be taken. The taxpayer should also be advised that an appeal of the matter may be made to the immediate manager.

(5) When an analysis of the taxpayer's financial condition shows that liquidation of assets and payments from present and future income will not result in full payment, consider the collection potential of an offer in compromise.

5225

Verification of Taxpayer's Financial Condition

(1) In some cases it will be necessary or desirable to obtain additional information about the taxpayer's financial condition. The extent of the investigation will depend upon the circumstances in each case.

(2) If items appear to be over- or understated, or out of the ordinary, the taxpayer should be asked to explain and substantiate if necessary. The explanation will be documented in the case history. If the explanation is unsatisfactory or cannot be substantiated, the amount should be revised appropriate to the documentation available.

5231.1

General Installment Agreement Guidelines

(1) When taxpayers state inability to pay the full amount of their taxes, installment agreements are to be considered.

(2) Future compliance with the tax laws will be addressed and any returns and/or tax due within the period of the agreement must be filed and paid timely.

(3) Levy source information, including complete addresses and ZIP codes, will be secured.

(4) Equal monthly installment payments should be requested. Payment amounts may be increased or decreased as necessary.

(5) Once the determination is made that the taxpayer has the capability to make a regular installment payment, that agreement will be monitored through routine provisions unless the payment amount is less than $10 (in which case the account should be reported currently not collectible). The major benefits of this approach are issuance of reminder and default notices (if the account is system-monitored) and enforcement action if the agreement is not kept.

(6) The taxpayer should be allowed to select the payment due date(s). But if there is no preference, the date when the taxpayer would generally be in the best financial position to make the payment(s) should be chosen.

(7) If the interviewer and the taxpayer cannot agree on the amount of installments, the taxpayer should be advised that an appeal may be made to the immediate manager.

(8) An installment agreement which lasts more than two years must be reviewed at the mid-point of the agreement, but in no event less than every two years.

Levy and Sale

5311

Introduction and General Concepts

(1)   Under the Internal Revenue Code, levy is defined as the power to collect taxes by distraint or seizure of the taxpayer's assets. Through levy, we can attach property in the possession of third parties or the taxpayer. Generally, a notice of levy is used to attach funds due the taxpayer from third parties. Levy on property in possession of the taxpayer is accomplished by seizure and public sale of the property. There is no statutory requirement as to the sequence to be followed in levying, but it is generally less burdensome and time consuming to levy on funds in possession of third parties.

(2)   Levy authority is far reaching. It permits a continuous attachment of the non-exempt portion of the wage or salary payments due the taxpayer, and the seizure and sale of all the taxpayer's assets except certain property that is specifically exempt by law. Prior to levying on any property belonging to a taxpayer, the Service must notify the taxpayer in writing of the Service's intention to levy. The statute does not require a judgment or other court order before levy action is taken. The Supreme Court decision in the matter of *G.M. Leasing Corporation v. United States,* 429 U.S. 338 (1977), held that an entry without a warrant and search of private areas of both residential and business premises for the purpose of seizing and inventorying property pursuant to Internal Revenue Code section 6331 is in violation of the Fourth Amendment. Prior to seizure of property on private premises, a consent to enter for the purpose of seizing or writ of entry from the local courts must be secured.

(3)   Procedures are designed (except in jeopardy cases) to give taxpayers a reasonable chance to settle their tax liabilities voluntarily before the more drastic enforcement actions are started. At least one final notice must be issued before service of a notice of levy.

(4)   Under the self-assessment system, a taxpayer is entitled to a reasonable opportunity to voluntarily comply with the revenue laws. This concept should also be followed in connection with levy action. This does not mean that there should be a

reluctance to levy if the circumstances justify that action. However, before levy or seizure is taken on an account, the taxpayer must be informed, except in jeopardy situations, that levy or seizure will be the next action taken and given a reasonable opportunity to pay voluntarily. Once the taxpayer has been advised and neglects to make satisfactory arrangements, levy action should be taken expeditiously, but not less than 10 days after notice.

(5) Notification prior to levy must be given in accordance with (2) above. It should be specific that levy action will be the next action taken. In the event the service center has not sent the taxpayer the 4th notice which includes notice of intention to levy at least 10 days before the levy, the revenue officer must provide the notice to the taxpayer as indicated in (2) above.

(6) A notice of levy should be served only when there is evidence or reasonable expectation that the third party has property or rights to property of the taxpayer. This concept is of particular significance, since processing of notices of levy is time consuming and often becomes a sensitive matter if it appears the levy action was merely a "fishing expedition."

5312

Statutory Authority to Levy

(1) IRC 6331 provides that if any person liable to pay any tax neglects or refuses to pay the tax within 10 days after notice and demand, the tax may be collected by levy upon any property or rights to property belonging to the taxpayer or on which there is a lien.

(2) IRC 6331 also provides that if the Secretary determines that the collection of tax is in jeopardy, immediate notice and demand for payment may be made and, upon the taxpayer's failure to pay the tax, collection may be made by levy without regard to the 10-day period. However, if a sale is required, a public notice of sale may not be issued within the 10-day period unless IRC 6336 (relating to sale of perishable goods) is applicable.

(3) Under the IRC, the term "property" includes all property or rights to property, whether real or personal, tangible or intangible. The term "tax" includes any

interest, additional amount, addition to tax, or assessable penalty, together with any cost that may accrue.

(4) Generally, property subject to a Federal tax lien which has been sold or otherwise transferred by the taxpayer, may be levied upon in the hands of the transferee or any subsequent transferee. However, there are exceptions for securities, motor vehicles and certain retail and casual sales.

(5) Levy may be made on any person in possession of, or obligated with respect to, property or rights to property subject to levy. These include, but are not necessarily limited to, receivables, bank accounts, evidences of debt, securities and accrued salaries, wages, commissions, and other compensation.

(6) The IRC does not require that property be seized in any particular sequence. Therefore, property may be levied upon regardless of whether it is real or personal, tangible or intangible, and regardless of which type of property is levied upon first.

(7) Whenever the proceeds from the levy on any property or rights to property are not sufficient to satisfy the tax liability, additional levies may be made upon the same property, or source of income or any other property or rights to property subject to levy, until the account is fully paid. However, further levies should be timed to avoid hardship to the taxpayer or his/her family.

5314.1

Property Exempt From Levy

(1) IRC 6334 enumerates the categories of property exempt from levy as follows.

(a) *Wearing apparel and school books necessary for the taxpayer or for members of his family*—No specific value limitation is placed on these items since the intent is to prevent seizing the ordinary clothing of the taxpayer or members of the family. Expensive items of wearing apparel, such as furs, are luxuries and are not exempt from levy.

(b) *Fuel, provisions and personal effects*—This exemption is applicable only in the case of the head of a family and applies only to so much of the fuel, provisions, furniture, and personal effects of the household and of arms for personal use, livestock, and poultry as does not exceed $1,500 in value.

(c) *Books and tools of a trade, business or profession*—This exemption is for so many of the books and tools necessary for the trade, business, or profession of the taxpayer as do not exceed in the aggregate $1,000 in value.

(d) *Unemployment benefits*—This applies to any amount payable to an individual for unemployment (including any portion payable to dependents) under an unemployment compensation law of the United States, any state, the District of Columbia or the Commonwealth of Puerto Rico.

(e) *Undelivered mail*—Addressed mail which has not been delivered to the addressee.

(f) *Certain annuity and pension payments.*

(g) *Workmen's compensation*—Any amount payable to an individual as workmen's compensation (including any portion payable to dependents) under a workmen's compensation law of the United States, any state, the District of Columbia, or the Commonwealth of Puerto Rico.

(h) *Judgment for support of minor children*—If the taxpayer is required by judgment of a court of competent jurisdiction, entered prior to the date of levy, to contribute to the support of his/her minor children, so much of his/her salary, wages, or other income as is necessary to comply with such judgment.

(i) *Minimum Exemption from Levy on Wages, Salary and Other Income*—IRC 6334(a)(9) limits the effect of levy on wages, salary and other income, by an amount of $75 per week for the taxpayer and an additional $25 a week for the spouse and each dependent claimed by the taxpayer. Income not paid or received on a weekly basis will, for the purpose of computing exemptions, be apportioned as if received on a weekly basis.

(2) In addition, Public Law 89-538 exempts deposits to the special Treasury fund made by servicemen and servicewomen (including officers) and Public Health Service employees on permanent duty assignment outside the United States or its possessions.

(3) Except for the exemptions in (1) and (2) above, no other property or rights to property are exempt from levy. No provision of state law can exempt property or rights to property from levy for the collection of federal taxes. The fact that property is exempt from execution under state personal or homestead exemption laws does not exempt the property from federal levy.

(4)   The revenue officer seizing property of the type described in (1)(a), (b), and (c) above should appraise and set aside to the owner the amount of property to be exempted.

538(10)

Records of Attorneys, Physicians, and Accountants

(1)   Records maintained by attorneys, physicians, and accountants concerning professional services performed for clients are usually of little intrinsic value and possess minimum sale value. Questions of confidential or privileged information contained in these records may cause complications if the records are seized. Additionally, the case files of the professional person frequently either are, or contain, property of the client, and therefore to this extent are not subject to seizure. Accordingly, it is not believed desirable to seize case files or records for payment of the taxpayer's tax liabilities.

(2)   When office facilities or office equipment of attorneys, physicians, or public accountants are seized for payment of taxes, case files and related files in seized office facilities or office equipment of such persons will not be personally examined by the revenue officer even though information concerning accounts receivable may be contained in the files. When storage facilities (filing cabinets, etc.) are seized, the taxpayer should be requested to remove all case files promptly.

583(11)

Safe Deposit Boxes

538(11).1

General

(1)   The procedures outlined below should be followed in an attempt to secure the opening of a taxpayer's safe deposit box in instances in which the taxpayer's consent to or cooperation in opening the box cannot be obtained.

(2)   Ordinarily two keys are used to open a safe deposit box: a master key held by the bank or trust company which owns the box and an individual key in the possession of the person who rents the box.

(3)   Irrespective of the possession of the necessary equipment to do so, it is not to be expected that a bank or trust company will open a safe deposit box without the consent of the lessee of the box unless protected by a court order. Under these circumstances the government must prevent the taxpayer from having access to the box, or obtain a court order directing that the box be opened, by force if necessary.

(4)   At the time that a safety deposit is secured, Publication 787, Seal for Securing Safety Deposit Boxes, will be signed by the revenue officer and affixed over the locks for security while the box remains under seizure. When the box is eventually opened, all residue from the seal should be removed by the revenue officer, or the bank official in the revenue officer's presence, with isopropyl alcohol or a similar solvent. To avoid damage to the safety deposit box, no sharp implement or abrasive substance should be used. The seal will dissolve when saturated with alcohol and rubbed with a cloth.

583(11).2

Preventing Access to Safe Deposit Box

(1)   A notice of lien should be filed prior to seizure since assets other than cash may be in the safe deposit box.

(2)   A notice of levy, Form 668-A, with a copy of the notice of lien attached, should be served on an officer of the bank or trust company and request made for surrender of the contents of the box.

(3)   The official may advise that the institution does not have the necessary key to open the safe deposit box or that the institution does not have the authority to open it. He/she may also suggest that the lessee's (taxpayer's) consent be secured, or that a court order be obtained to open the box.

(4)   Under these circumstances, the revenue officer should not insist that the box be opened and no attempt should be made to have the box opened by force. The box should be sealed by affixing a seizure notice, Publication 787, Seal for Securing Safety Deposit Boxes. It should be placed over the locks in such a manner so that the box cannot be opened without removing, tearing or destroying the affixed seal. The bank or trust company should then be advised not to permit the box to be opened except in the presence of a revenue officer.

(5)   Usually, taxpayers who have been reluctant to cooperate will eventually find it necessary to open their boxes, and will only be able to do so in the presence of a revenue officer. At that time, the revenue officer, with Form 668-B in his/her possession, will be in a position to seize any property in the box.

(6)   When the rental period of the safe deposit box expires and is not renewed, a bank or trust company usually has the right and power to open the box. The revenue officer should attempt to ascertain the true situation in any given case, and if the right and power exists, should try to take advantage of this opportunity to seize the contents of the box.

538(11).3

Obtaining Court Order To Open

(1)   Occasionally, the procedure outlined in IRM 538(11).2 will not be satisfactory and immediate action may be desirable or necessary. For instance, the statute of limitations may be about to expire, the taxpayer may have disappeared or be in concealment, or the taxpayer or bank officials may refuse cooperation and deny access to a safe deposit box.

(2)   Under these circumstances a Summons should be prepared and served on the taxpayer-boxholder in an attempt to secure information as to the contents of the box and to gain access. If this action does not accomplish the desired results, a writ of entry should be sought or a suit requested to open the safe deposit box.

Currently Not Collectible Accounts

5610

Determination of Currently Not Collectible Taxes

5611

General

(1) A Collection employee may determine that the accounts are currently not collectible.

(2) Reporting an account currently not collectible does not abate the assessment. It only stops current efforts to collect it. Collection can start again any time before the statutory period for collection expires.

5632

Unable-To-Pay Cases—Hardship

5632.1

General

(1) If collection of the liability would prevent the taxpayer from meeting necessary living expenses, it may be reported currently not collectible under a hardship closing code. Sometimes accounts should be reported currently not collectible even though the Collection Information Statement (CIS) shows assets or sources of income subject to levy.

   (a) [The Manual] provides guidelines for analyzing the taxpayer's financial condition.
   (b) Since each taxpayer's circumstances are unique, other factors such as age and health must be considered as appropriate.
   (c) Document and verify the taxpayer's financial condition.
   (d) Consider the collection potential of an offer in compromise.

(2) Consider an installment agreement before reporting an account currently not collectible as hardship.

Offers in Compromise

5712

Grounds for Compromise

5712.1

General Guidelines

The compromise of a tax liability can only rest upon doubt as to liability, doubt as to collectibility, or doubt as to both liability and collectibility. IRC 7122 does not confer authority to compromise tax, interest, or penalty where the liability is clear and there is no doubt as to the ability of the Government to collect. To compromise there must be room for mutual concessions involving either or both doubt as to liability or doubt as to ability to pay. This rules out, as ground for compromise, equity or public policy considerations peculiar to a particular case, individual hardships, and similar matters which do not have a direct bearing on liability or ability to pay.

5713.2

Advising Taxpayers of Offer Provisions

(1)   When criminal proceedings are not contemplated and an analysis of taxpayer's assets, liabilities, income and expenses shows that a liability cannot realistically be paid in full in the foreseeable future, the collection potential of an offer in compromise should be considered. While it is difficult to outline the exact circumstances when an offer would be the appropriate collection tool, the existence of any of the following should govern offer consideration.

   (a)   Liquidation of assets and payments from present and future income will not result in full payment of tax liability.

   (b)   A non-liable spouse has property which he/she may be interested in utilizing to secure a compromise of spouse's tax debt.

   (c)   The taxpayer has an interest in assets against which collection action cannot be taken. For example, the taxpayer who owes a separate liability, has an interest in property held in "tenancy by the entirety" which cannot be reached or subjected to the Notice of Federal Tax Lien because of the provisions of state law. Under the compromise procedures, the taxpayer's interest is included in the total assets available in arriving at an acceptable offer in compromise.

(d) The taxpayer has relatives or friends who may be willing to lend or give the taxpayer funds for the sole purpose of reaching a compromise with the Service.

5721

General

The offer in compromise is the taxpayer's written proposal to the Government and, if accepted, is an agreement enforceable by either party under the law of contracts. Therefore, it must be definite in its terms and conditions, since it directly affects the satisfaction of the tax liability.

5723.1

Prescribed Form

A taxpayer seeking to compromise a tax liability based on doubt as to collectibility must submit Form 433, Statement of Financial Condition and Other Information. This form includes questions geared to develop a full and complete description of the taxpayer's financial situation.

5723.3

Refusal To Submit Financial Statement

If a taxpayer professing inability to pay refuses to submit the required Form 433, the offer will be immediately rejected since the Service cannot determine whether the amount offered is also the maximum amount collectible.

5725.1

Liability of Husband and Wife

(1) Under IRC 6013(d)(3), the liability for income tax on a joint return by husband and wife is expressly made "joint and several." Either or both of the spouses are liable for the entire amount of the tax shown on a joint return. When the liability of both parties is sought to be compromised, the offer should be submitted in the names of

and signed by both spouses in order to make the waiver and other provisions of the offer form effective against both parties.

(2) An "innocent spouse" may be relieved of liability in certain cases under IRC 6013(e) and IRC 6653(b). In the event that one of the jointly liable taxpayers claims to be an "innocent spouse," the question should be referred to the district Examination function for determination.

   (a) Should the offer be acceptable, the report should not be prepared until after the district Examination function has made its determination. Since a favorable decision for the party claiming "innocent spouse" will change the amount of the liability sought to be compromised, any recommendation for acceptance must reflect the redetermined liability.

5740

Investigation of Offers

5741.1

General

(1) Once an offer in compromise is received in Special Procedures function, a determination whether the offer merits further consideration must be made. SPf should use all information contained in the offer file and may consult with the revenue officer assigned the TDAs [tax deficiency assessments] to obtain additional financial information or verify existing information.

(2) Summary rejection in SPf can be made on the grounds that the offer is frivolous, was filed merely to delay collection, or where there is no basis for compromise. A desk review of the offer can result in this determination. Although not all-inclusive, the following list provides guidelines on the criteria for summary rejection most often encountered:

   (a) Taxpayer has equity in assets subject to the Federal tax lien clearly in excess of the total liability sought to be compromised,

   (b) The total liability is extremely large and the taxpayer has offered only a minimum sum well below his/her equity and earning potential (e.g., offering $100 to compromise a $50,000 tax liability). Although the taxpayer could be persuaded to raise the offer, the fact that this initial amount offered was so low indicates bad faith and the desire to delay collection,

(c) The taxpayer is not current in his/her filing or payment requirements for periods not included in the offer,

(d) The taxpayer refuses to submit a complete financial statement (Form 433),

(e) Acceptance of the offer would adversely affect the image of the government,

(f) Taxpayer has submitted a subsequent offer which is not significantly different from a previously rejected offer and the taxpayer's financial condition has not changed,

(g) In cases involving doubt as to liability for the 100-percent penalty, the liability is clearly established and the taxpayer has offered no new evidence to cast doubt on its validity.

5741.2

Public Policy

(1) An accepted offer, like any contract, is an agreement between two parties resulting from a "meeting of the minds." It is incumbent upon each party to negotiate the best terms possible. Normally, the offer and subsequent negotiations are of a private nature. However, when accepting an offer, the Service is in a unique position since it represents the government's interest in the negotiations and the accepted offer becomes part of public record. Therefore, public policy dictates that an offer can be rejected if public knowledge of the agreement is detrimental to the government's interest. The offer may be rejected even though it can be shown conclusively that the amounts offered are greater than could reasonably be collected in any other manner. Because the Government would be in the position of foregoing revenue, the circumstances in which public policy considerations could be used to reject the offer must be construed very strictly. The following may be used as a guideline for instances where public policy issues are most often encountered:

(a) Taxpayer's notoriety is such that acceptance of an offer will hamper future Service collection and/or compliance efforts. However, simply because the taxpayer is famous or well-known is not a basis in and of itself for rejecting the offer on public policy grounds.

(b)   There is a possibility of establishing a precedent which might lead to numerous offers being submitted on liabilities incurred as a result of occupational drives to enforce tax compliance.

(c)   Taxpayer has been recently convicted of tax related crimes. Again, the notoriety of the individual should be considered when making a public policy determination. The publicity surrounding the case, taxpayer's compliance since the case was concluded, or the taxpayer's position in the community should all be considered prior to rejecting an otherwise acceptable offer.

(d)   Situations where it is suspected that the financial benefits of criminal activity are concealed or the criminal activity is continuing would normally preclude acceptance of the offer for public policy reasons. Criminal Investigation function should be contacted to coordinate the Government's action in these cases.

Bankruptcy for Wage Earners– A Positive Option

5

In these difficult economic times, all forms of bankruptcy filings have increased dramatically. However, many people are unaware of the the Wage Earner Plan and how it can work to help them. The Wage Earner Plan was designed by Congress to allow an individual to reorganize his or her debts without losing all of his or her assets, as is the case in a bankruptcy filed under Chapter 7 of the Bankruptcy Code. The Wage Earner Plan allows individuals the same opportunity that the largest corporations enjoy—reorganization.

Many people may feel they will be stigmatized or embarrassed by a bankruptcy filing. That attitude simply is not justified. A casual review of your daily newspaper will reveal that some of the largest corporations, prominent entertainers, sports figures and even attorneys have all used the bankruptcy laws to put themselves back on level ground. Obviously, they did not feel stigmatized. Even though bankruptcy is a public matter,

you would be surprised at how many of your neighbors are benefitting by a bankruptcy.

Conceptually and in practice, a Wage Earner Plan is uncomplicated. It is a court-sanctioned approach to sound debt management, i.e., living within an allowance by developing a budget.

A Wage Earner Plan provides you with many of the benefits of debt consolidation without the detriments of loans. Those benefits include:

1. During the term of the plan, there are generally no interest charges for pre-existing debts;

2. With the approval of the Court, you establish the amount you are willing and able to pay periodically to creditors;

3. With the approval of the Court, you determine the amount your creditors will receive under the Plan.

How the Process Works

A Wage Earner Plan or Chapter 13 case is launched with the filing of a Bankruptcy Petition. The Petition is filed with the Clerk of the Bankruptcy Court. The Petition is a disclosure form that shows the Court how you have budgeted your living expenses and how you propose to repay your creditors. It will contain your personal financial statement and show the portion of your income that is available to pay creditors after your living expenses are paid.

The commencement of any bankruptcy case stops all collection actions dead in their tracks. Further, other than support obligations, any wage attachments or garnishments are invalidated. All future payments to creditors will be made by your court-appointed Trustee.

Shortly after the filing of your petition, you must attend a meeting of your creditors conducted by the Trustee. This meeting will take place from one to six months after the filing of the petition. At the meeting the Trustee will ask you, under oath, about your petition and your finances. It is the Trustee's responsibility to determine the likelihood of a successful reorganization.

If the Trustee determines that the plan has a likelihood of success, he will recommend that the Judge confirm the Plan. At this point you will meet with the Judge, and the Plan will be effective upon confirmation.

Who Can Use a Chapter 13 Wage Earners Plan

Section 103(e) of the Bankruptcy Code identifies the persons who may take advantage of a Chapter 13, Wage Earner Plan, reorganization effort. You must be an individual "with regular income that owes, on the date of filing the petition, noncontingent, liquidated, unsecured debts of less than $100,000 and noncontingent, liquidated, unsecured debts of less than $350,000." Further, you must be an individual residing in or having a domicile in the United States, and you must have a regular income. The regular income requirement is satisfied if your "income is sufficiently stable and regular" for you to be able to make payments under the plan.

Determining the Chapter 13 Plan

The largest hurdle you will face in your Chapter 13 efforts is creating your payment plan. Remember, it is possible that some debts will be discharged without payment in full. The balancing task requires you to recognize that:

1.   In general, a Chapter 13 should be completed within 3 years; and

2.   All unsecured creditors must receive what they would have received had you chosen a Chapter 7 complete liquidation plan.

In determining your plan, first identify the property that is subject to the bankruptcy and the property that is exempt. "Exempt property" is defined by statute. You may choose either the amounts granted under the federal bankruptcy code or your state's exemptions. There is no rule of thumb. Each state's exemptions differ, and you must carefully check your state's law before choosing.

For example, as will be explained in Chapter 6, pension funds are not exempt from bankruptcy under federal law. However, some states grant an exemption to pensions, i.e., Pennsylvania. In contrast, New Jersey does not exempt pensions. Therefore, in a Pennsylvania bankruptcy, the value of your pension would not be included in determining the amount to be paid under the bankruptcy plan, while in New Jersey it would.

Having identified and elected the correct exemption, all other property you own is non-exempt. The value of your non-exempt property is the minimum that your plan must pay out. Remember, for a Chapter 13 to be "confirmed," the unsecured creditors must receive at least what they would have had you liquidated your assets under Chapter 7.

Dischargeable Debts

Most of your debts are dischargeable in a Chapter 13 bankruptcy. Discharge means the debt is extinguished and completely satisfied. But not all of your debts are dischargeable. Nondischargeable debts include:

1. Child support and alimony.

2. Debts not disclosed in your bankruptcy filing.

3. Restitution that is ordered because of criminal activity.

4. Debts obtained through either fraud or deceit.

5. Debts resulting from willful or malicious injury.

6. Debts on which final payment is due after the final date of the plan.

7. Debts that are reaffirmed after the confirmation of the plan.

8. Penalties and fines due for tax liabilities.

9. Certain tax liabilities, such as employment taxes.

10. Student loans.

In general, all other debts you may have incurred are dischargeable. That is, they will be wiped out after your plan has been completed.

Some Questions Concerning Chapter 13

Q. How do Chapter 13 and Chapter 7 bankruptcies differ?

A. A Chapter 7 is a complete liquidation, whereas a Chapter 13 is a "reorganization" and work-out of your debts. In a Chapter 7 you will lose all of your non-exempt property which will be sold by the trustee. The proceeds will be given to your creditors, and you will be completely discharged of your debts. In a Chapter 13 you keep all of your assets, both exempt and non-exempt. Your plan will pay off all the debts to the extent that the court determines possible, and the remainder of your debts will be discharged.

Q. How often may I file for bankruptcy?

A. You may file a Chapter 7 bankruptcy only once in six years. A Chapter 13 may be filed repeatedly; however, there is a six-month waiting period required between filings.

Q. What are the Chapter 13 fees?

A. The filing fee is $120. Further, the

Trustee receives a fee equal to ten percent (10%) of the total payments paid under the plan. If your plan requires $20,000 in plan payments, the total fees would be $120 filing fee plus $2,000 trustee fee for a total of $2,120.

Q. How long will a Chapter 13 plan last?

A. In general, a Wage Earner Plan runs for three years. The plan may last as long as five years and, if all debts can be paid in less time, the plan can be shorter than three years.

Q. Can I have too much debt to qualify for a Chapter 13?

A. Yes, if you have unsecured debts that are liquidated or noncontingent and they exceed $100,000, or if you have secured debts that are liquidated or noncontingent and they exceed $350,000, you will not be allowed to file a Chapter 13 bankruptcy.

Q. What happens to guarantees or co-signed debts?

A. First, we must distinguish between

consumer debt and business debt. In general, if the debt is a consumer debt to be fully paid during the Chapter 13, the creditor will not go against the co-signer or guarantor. However, if the debt is a business debt or is a consumer debt that will not be fully paid under the plan, the creditor can make the co-signer pay.

Q. Will I lose any property by filing a Chapter 13 plan?

A. Normally, no. The idea of the plan is to grant you time to "catch up" on your obligations. Debts are paid from income you receive after the filing of the bankruptcy. You may, however, lose some property if your nonexempt property is valuable and you would not otherwise pay to your creditors what they would receive if you liquidated your property.

Q. Will my filing be public?

A. Yes. The filing of a bankruptcy is public record. Many legal newspapers and most general circulation newspapers will print a list of bankruptcies.

Q. Does my employer have to know that I filed for bankruptcy?

A. Generally, the court, through the Trustee, will contact your employer to either verify your income or to make arrangements for the payment of your income directly to the Trustee in order to make plan payments.

Q. Can I be fired or discriminated against by my employer for filing bankruptcy?

A. No. It is a crime for any employer to discriminate against individuals for filing of a bankruptcy. However, some bonded positions, like security guards, stock brokers and casino cashiers, may have some difficulty. In those circumstances, you must discuss your situation with your employer. Open and frank talk should satisfy their fears.

Q. Must I repay all of my debts?

A. No. You are only required, subject to court approval, to repay only as much of your debt as your creditors would have received if you liquidated all of your non-exempt property.

Q. Should a husband and wife file a plan jointly?

A. If both husband and wife have significant debts, they should file a joint plan. The only requirement is that at least one of them must have sufficient income and that their joint debts do not exceed the dollar limits. In some states, those that recognize tenants by the entireties, it may be beneficial not to file a joint plan. The entireties property may be exempt from the bankruptcy if only one spouse files, whereas the entireties property will be subject to the bankruptcy if both spouses file jointly.

Q. How does a Chapter 13 affect my credit history?

A. At first, the filing may result in a worsening of your credit rating. Remember, credit agencies will report the bankruptcy on your file for up to ten years. However, if your debts are substantially paid off under the plan, many creditors will take that into account and treat you as one who has rehabilitated his or her credit.

How to File a Plan by Yourself

You do not need to use an attorney to file a Chapter 13 bankruptcy. The bankruptcy is started with the filing of the Petition (see forms attached) and the payment of the filing fee of $120.00. The petition and bankruptcy forms are generally the same throughout the United States; however, the local District court may have chosen its own style for local rules. Check with the clerk of your local bankruptcy court. Although the clerks do not give "legal" advice, they are usually helpful and will aid you in your efforts to comply with local requirements.

The procedure is quite straightforward:

1. Get a set of bankruptcy forms from your local legal supply store or office stationery store. Most come as preprinted packages that have the correct number of carbon copies included.

2. You must type the forms. Neatness does count. The clerk of the court will not accept improperly completed forms. If you need additional space to complete a schedule, use white paper and title it with the same name as the form you are continuing. You can expect to complete most of the listed forms:

    a. Voluntary petition
    b. Chapter 13 statement
    c. Chapter 13 plan and related schedules (check with the clerk to see if local forms are provided)
    d. Address matrix sheet

3. Deliver the forms with the filing fee of $120 to the clerk of the bankruptcy court. The number of copies you will need is determined by the local court. Check with the clerk prior to wasting a trip to court. Generally, five (5) copies will be enough.

4. The clerk will time stamp a copy for you. This is your receipt. It should contain the case number assigned by the court; however, some courts are backlogged, and the clerk may not be able to issue your case number when you file. If this happens, contact the court within a few days to get your case number.

5. If you are subject to a garnishment, contact both your employer and the creditor attaching your wages as soon as you have made your filing. The filing stops all forms of collection during the bankruptcy. A creditor may be held in contempt if it continues to try to collect after it has been notified of the bankruptcy.

6. Keep your case number handy. The court will notify your creditors, but you can speed things along by advising your creditors and collection agencies of your bankruptcy. They will need your case number.

7. Keep the court advised of your address in the event you move. Now you just have to wait for the process to go forward. Good Luck!

PROPERTY EXEMPTIONS
UNDER THE FEDERAL
BANKRUPTCY ACT

TYPE OF PROPERTY EXEMPTED	STATUTES CREATING THE EXEMPTIONS	MAXIMUM AMOUNT EXEMPTED
Real or Personal Property used as a residence (includes Mobile Home) or a Burial Plot.	11 U.S.C. §522(d)(1)	$7,500.00
One Motor Vehicle.	11 U.S.C. §522(d)(2)	1,200.00
All items of household furnishings, goods and appliances.	11 U.S.C. §522(d)(3) (per item)* (See No. 1 below)	200.00
All items of wearing apparel.	11 U.S.C. §522(d)(3) (per item)* (See No. 1 below)	200.00
All items of: Books, Animals, Crops or Musical Instruments	11 U.S.C. §522(d)(3) (per item)* (See No. 1 below)	200.00
Jewelry (total value of all pieces)	11 U.S.C. §522(d)(4)	500.00
Professional Books, Tools of Trade and Implements	11 U.S.C. §522(d)(6)	750.00
Professionally prescribed Health Aids.	11 U.S.C. §522(d)(9)	any amount
Social Security Benefits, Unemployment Compensation, Public Assistance, Veterans Benefits, Alimony, Support, Separate Maintenance, Payments under a Stock Plan, Profit Sharing Plan, Annuity or other plan for the reason of illness, disability, death, age or length of service.	11 U.S.C. §522(d)(10)	any amount
An Award under the Crime Victims Reparation Law	11 U.S.C. §522(11)(A)	any amount
Life Insurance payments when debtor is the dependent of the insured.	11 U.S.C. §522(d)(11)(C)	any amount
A payment for the wrongful death of an individual of whom debtor was a dependent.	11 U.S.C. §522(d)(11)(B)	any amount
A payment for loss of future earnings of a debtor or an individual upon who debtor is dependent	11 U.S.C. §522(d)(11)(E)	any amount
Debtor's interest in any other property not particularly itemized in this Schedule	11 U.S.C. §522(d)(5)* (See No. 2 below)	400.00
A portion of the amounts not used under Section 522(d)(1) above to exempt Real or Personal property used as a residence or burial plot may be used under this statute to exempt any other property whether or not such property has been previously claimed under a previous statute.[2]	11 U.S.C. §522(d)(5)* (See No. 2 below)	3,750.00

NOTE: Under the 1984 amendments to the Bankruptcy Code, husband and wife debtors cannot claim separate exemptions under both the Federal Exemption Laws and the State Statutes. In other words, they must both claim their exemptions under the same set of laws. This is, of course, assuming that the Federal Exemption Laws apply in the State where you plan to file your action

---

[1]The maximum amount that can be exempted under this Section 522(d)(3) is an aggregate total of $4,000.00.

[2]Under this statute, any amount left over (not exceeding $3,750.00) after applying the allowed exemption to a residence or burial plot can be used to exempt other property whether previously exempted or not scheduled. For example, Boats, Airplanes, Income tax refunds, exempt wages, etc.

Exempt Property Under Other Federal Laws

There are various Federal Laws, other than the Federal Bankruptcy Laws, that provide for the exemption of certain property. These exemptions, as scheduled below, can be used in a Bankruptcy Action if there does not exist an applicable State or Federal Bankruptcy Exemption Statute which specifically exempts the possessed property. An example of this application is: (1) Income received under the Social Security Act, (2) Railroad Retirement Act, (3) Federal Civil Service Retirement Act, etc.

Property Exempted	Federal Statute
The earnings of a debtor subject to process is limited to a maximum of 25% of disposable earnings.	15 U.S.C. § 1673
Railroad Employees Retirement Benefits under the Railroad Retirement Act.	45 U.S.C. § 228(L)
All lands acquired by Federal Homestead Laws.	43 U.S.C. § 175
All Veterans Administration proceeds, including Veterans pensions, U.S. Life Insurance Benefits, pensions and disability allowances.	38 U.S.C. § 3101
Any and all benefits under the Social Security Act.	42 U.S.C. § 407
Retirement benefits under the Federal Civil Service or Employees Retirement Fund.	5 U.S.C. § 8346

CHAPTER 13 PETITION
AND SCHEDULES

UNITED STATES BANKRUPTCY COURT FOR THE   DISTRICT OF _____

Date Petition Filed _____
Case Number _____
Bankruptcy Judge _____

In re

_____

Debtor*

}

CHAPTER 13
VOLUNTARY PETITION
& EXHIBIT "B"

Soc. Sec. No. _____   Debtor's Employer's Tax Id. No. _____

(If this form is used for joint petitioners wherever the word "petitioner" or words referring to petitioner are used they shall be read as if in the plural.)

1. Petitioner's mailing address, including county, is

2. Petitioner has   ☐   resided within this district for the preceding 180 days.
                     ☐   had his(*her*) domicile within this district for the preceding 180 days.
                     ☐   had his(*her*) principal place of business within this district for the preceding 180 days.
                     ☐   had his(*her*) principal assets within this district for the preceding 180 days.
                     ☐   resided or been domiciled or had his(*her*) principal place of business within this district for a
                          longer portion of the preceding 180 days than in any other district.

3. Petitioner is qualified to file this petition and is entitled to the benefits of title 11, United States Code as a voluntary
debtor.

4.   ☐ A copy of petitioner's proposed plan, dated _____   19 _____   is attached.
     ☐ Petitioner intends to file a plan pursuant to chapter 13 of title 11, United States Code.

5.   A declaration in the form of Exhibit "B" is attached to and made a part of this petition.[1]

Wherefore, petitioner prays for relief in accordance with chapter 13 of title 11, United States Code.

Petitioner(s) signs if not represented by attorney

Signed: _____
                    Attorney for Petitioner

Address: _____

_____

_____
                         Petitioner

_____
                         Petitioner

DECLARATION

INDIVIDUAL: I, _____   the petitioner named in the
foregoing petition, declare under penalty of perjury under the laws of the United States that the foregoing is true and correct.

JOINT INDIVIDUALS: We, _____   and _____
the petitioners named in the foregoing petition, declare under penalty of perjury under the laws of the United States that the
foregoing is true and correct.

Executed on _____   19 _____   Signature: _____
                                                                    Petitioner

_____
                         Petitioner

EXHIBIT "B"

I, _____   the attorney for the petitioner named in the
foregoing petition, declare that I have informed the petitioner that he or she may proceed under chapter 7 or 13 of title 11,
United State Code, and have explained the relief available under each such chapter.

Executed on _____   Signature of Attorney for Petitioner _____

*Set forth here all names including tradenames used by Debtor within last 6 years.

[1]This paragraph applies if petitioner is an individual whose debts are primarily consumer debts and petitioner is represented by an attorney, otherwise delete.

In re

}

CHAPTER 13
STATEMENT

Debtor*

Soc. Sec. No.   Debtor's Employer's Tax Id. No.

(If this form is used by joint debtors wherever the word "debtor" or words referring to debtor are used they shall be read as if in the plural.)

     Each question shall be answered or the failure to answer explained. If the answer is "none" or "not applicable" so state. If additional space is needed for the answer to any question, a separate sheet, properly identified and made a part hereof, should be used and attached.
     The term, "original petition," used in the following questions, shall mean the original petition filed under § 301 of the Code or, if the chapter 13 case was converted from another chapter of the Code, shall mean the petition by or against you which originated the first case.
     This form must be completed in full whether a single or a joint petition is filed. When information is requested for "each" or "either spouse filing a petition" it should be supplied for both when a joint petition is filed.

| 1. **Name and residence** | (b) Where does debtor, if single, or each spouse filing a petition now reside? | (3) Telephone number |
| (a) Give full name | (1) Mailing address, (2) City or town, state and zip code | including area code |

Husband [or, *if single*, Debtor]

Wife

     (c) What does debtor, if single, or each spouse filing a petition consider his or her residence, if different from that listed in (b) above?
         Husband [*or* Debtor]

         Wife

2. **Occupation and income** (a) Give present occupation of debtor, if single, or each spouse filing a petition. (If more than one, list all for debtors or each spouse filing a petition.)
         Husband [*or* Debtor]

         Wife

     (b)   What is the name, address, and telephone number of present employer (or employers) of debtor, if single, or each spouse filing a petition? (Include also any identifying badge or card number with employer.)
         Husband [*or* Debtor]

         Wife

     (c)   How long has debtor, if single, or each spouse filing a petition been employed by present employer?
         Husband [or Debtor]   Wife

     (d)   If debtor or either spouse filing a petition has not been employed by present employer for a period of 1 year, state the name of prior employer(s) and nature of employment during that period.
         Husband [*or* Debtor]

         Wife

     (e)   Has debtor or either spouse filing a petition operated a business, in partnership or otherwise, during the past 3 years? (If so, give the particulars, including names, dates, and places.)
         Husband [*or* Debtor]

         Wife

(f) Answer the following questions for debtor, if single, or each spouse whether single or joint petition is filed unless spouses are separated and a single petition is filed:

(1) What are your gross wages, salary or commissions per pay period?

	Husband [or Debtor]	Wife
(a) Weekly	$ _____	$ _____
(b) Semi-monthly	$ _____	$ _____
(c) Monthly	$ _____	$ _____
(d) Other (specify)	$ _____	$ _____

(2) What are your payroll deductions per pay period for?

	Husband [or Debtor]	Wife
(a) Payroll taxes (including social security)	$ _____	$ _____
(b) Insurance	$ _____	$ _____
(c) Credit union	$ _____	$ _____
(d) Union dues	$ _____	$ _____
(e) Other (specify)	$ _____	$ _____
(f) _____	$ _____	$ _____
(g) _____	$ _____	$ _____

(3) What is your take-home pay per period?   Husband [or Debtor]$_____   Wife $_____

(4) What was the amount of your gross income for the last calendar year?   Husband [or Debtor] $_____   Wife $_____

(5) Is your employment subject to seasonal or other change?   Husband [or Debtor] $_____   Wife $_____

(6) Has either of you made any wage assignments or allotments? (If so, indicate which spouse's wages assigned or allotted, the name and address of the person to whom assigned or allotted, and the amount owing, if any, to such person. If allotment or assignment is to a creditor, the claim should also be listed in Item 11a.)

3. **Dependents** (To be answered by debtor if unmarried, otherwise for each spouse whether single or joint petition is filed unless spouses are separated and a single petition is filed.)

(a) Does either of you pay [or receive] alimony, maintenance or support?   If so, how much per month?
For whose support? (Give name, age, and relationship to you.)

   Husband [or Debtor]

   Wife

(b) List all other dependents, other than present spouse, not listed in (a) above. (Give name, age, and relationship to you.)

   Husband [or Debtor]

   Wife

4. **Budget** (*a*) Give your estimated average future monthly income if unmarried, otherwise for each spouse whether single or joint petition is filed, unless spouses are separated and a single petition is filed.

    (1) Husband's (or Debtor's) monthly take-home pay _____ $ _____

    (2) Wife's monthly take-home pay_____ $ _____

    (3) Other monthly income (specify) _____ $ _____

    (4) _____ $ _____

    (5) _____ $ _____

    (6) _____ $ _____

    (7) _____ Total $ _____

(*b*) Give estimated average future monthly expenses of family (not including debts to be paid under plan), consisting of:

    (1) Rent or home mortgage payment (include lot rental for trailer) _____ $ _____

    (2) Utilities (Electricity $ _____   Heat $ _____   Water $ _____   Telephone $ _____) $ _____

    (3) Food_____ $ _____

    (4) Clothing_____ $ _____

    (5) Laundry and cleaning_____ $ _____

    (6) Newspapers, periodicals, and books (including school books) _____ $ _____

    (7) Medical and drug expenses_____ $ _____

    (8) Insurance (not deducted from wages): (a) Auto $ _____   (b) Other $ _____ $ _____

    (9) Transportation (not including auto payments to be paid under plan) _____ $ _____

    (10) Recreation _____ $ _____

    (11) Dues, union, professional, social or otherwise (not deducted from wages) _____ $ _____

    (12) Taxes (not deducted from wages) _____ $ _____

    (13) Alimony, maintenance, or support payments _____ $ _____

    (14) Other payments for support of dependents not living at home _____ $ _____

    (15) Other (specify):_____ $ _____

            _____ $ _____

            _____ $ _____

            _____ $ _____

            _____ $ _____

            _____ $ _____

            _____ Total $ _____

(*c*) Excess of estimated future monthly income (last line of Item 4(a) above) over estimated future exp. (last line of Item 4(b) above) _____ $ _____

(*d*) Total amount to be paid each month under plan _____ $ _____

5. **Payment of attorney**

    (*a*) How much have you agreed to pay or what property have you agreed to transfer to your attorney in connection with this case? _____ $ _____

    (*b*) How much have you paid or what have you transferred to the attorney? _____ $ _____

6. **Tax refunds*** To what tax refunds (income or other), if any, is either of you, or may either of you be entitled? (Give particulars, including information as to any refunds payable jointly to you or any other person. All such refunds should also be listed in Item 13(b).)

7. **Financial accounts, certificates of deposit and safe deposit boxes***

   (a) Does either of you currently have any accounts or certificates of deposit or shares in banks, savings and loan, thrift, building and loan and homestead associations, credit unions, brokerage houses, pension funds and the like? (If so, give name and address of each institution, number and nature of account, current balance, and name and address of every other person authorized to make withdrawals from the account. Such accounts should also be listed in Item 13(b).)

   (b) Does either of you currently keep any safe deposit boxes or other depositories? (If so, give name and address of bank or other depository, name and address of every other person who has a right of access thereto, and a brief description of the contents thereof, which should also be listed in Item 13(b).)

8. **Prior Bankruptcy** What proceedings under the Bankruptcy Act or Bankruptcy Code have previously been brought by or against you or either spouse filing a petition? (State the location of the bankruptcy court, the nature and number of each proceeding, the date when it was filed, and whether a discharge was granted or denied, the proceeding was dismissed, or a composition, arrangement, or plan was confirmed.)

9. **Foreclosures, executions, and attachments*** (a) Is any of the property of either of you, including real estate, involved in a foreclosure proceeding, in or out of court? (If so, identify the property and the person foreclosing.)

   (b) Has any property or income of either of you been attached, garnished, or seized under any legal or equitable process within the 90 days immediately preceding the filing of the original petition herein? (If so, describe the property seized, or person garnished, and at whose suit.)

10. **Repossessions and returns*** Has any property of either of you been returned to, repossessed, or seized by the seller or by any other party, including a landlord, during the 90 days immediately preceding the filing of the original petition herein? (If so, give particulars, including the name and address of the party taking the property and its description and value.)

11. **Transfers of Property*** *(a)* Has either of you made any gifts, other than ordinary and usual presents to family members and charitable donations, during the year immediately preceding the filing of the original petition herein? (If so, give names and addresses of donees and dates, description and value of gifts.)

    (b) Has either of you made any other transfer, absolute or for the purpose of security, or any other disposition, of real or personal property during the year immediately preceding the filing of the original petition herein? (Give a description of the property, the date of the transfer or disposition, to whom transferred or how disposed of, and, if the transferee is a relative or insider, the relationship, the consideration, if any, received therefor, and the disposition of such consideration.)

12. **Debts** (To be answered by debtor, if unmarried, otherwise for each spouse whether single or joint petition is filed.)

    (a) *Debts Having Priority.*

(1) Nature of claim	(2) Name of creditor and complete mailing address, including zip code	(3) Specify when claim was incurred and the consideration therefor: when claim is subject to setoff, evidenced by a judgment, negotiable instrument, or other writing	(4) Indicate if claim is contingent, unliquidated, or disputed	(5) M(D) W or J	(6) Amount of claim
1. Wages, salary, and commissions, including vacation, severance and sick leave pay owing to employees not exceeding $2,000 to each, earned within 90 days before filing of petition or cessation of business (if earlier specify date).					$
2. Contributions to employee benefit plans for services rendered within 180 days before filing of petition or cessation of business (if earlier specify date).					
3. Deposits by individuals, not exceeding $900 for each for purchase, lease, or rental of property or services for personal, family, or household use that were not delivered or provided.					
4. Taxes owing (itemize by type of tax and taxing authority) (A) To the United States (B) To any state (C) To any other taxing authority					
				Total	

    (b) *Secured Debts.*—List all debts which are or may be secured by real or personal property. (Indicate in sixth column, if debt payable in installments, the amount of each installment, the installment period (Monthly, weekly, or otherwise) and number of installments in arrears, if any. Indicate in the last column whether husband or wife solely liable, or whether you are jointly liable.)

Creditor's name, account number and complete mailing address. Including zip code	Consideration or basis for debt	Amount claimed by creditor	If disputed, amount admitted by debtor	Description of collateral (include year and make of automobile)	Installment amount, period, and number of installments in arrears	Husband or wife solely liable, or jointly liable

Total secured debts $ _____

12. Debts (Continued)

(c) *Unsecured Debts.*—List all other debts, liquidated and unliquidated, including taxes, attorneys' fees and tort claims.

Creditor's name, account number and complete mailing address, including zip code	Consideration or basis for debt	Amount claimed by creditor	If disputed, amount admitted by debtor	Husband or wife solely liable, or jointly liable

(a)	Total debts having priority	$ _____
(b)	Total secured debts	$ _____
(c)	Total unsecured debts	$ _____
	Total (a) + (b) + (c)	$ _____

13. Codebtors (To be answered by debtor, if unmarried, otherwise for each spouse whether single or joint petition is filed.)

(a) Are any other persons liable, as cosigners, guarantors or in any other manner, on any of the debts of either of you or is either of you so liable on the debts of others? (If so, give particulars, indicating which spouse liable and including names of creditors, nature of debt, names and addresses of codebtors, and their relationship, if any, to you.)

(b) If so, have the codebtors made any payments on the debts? (Give name of each codebtor and amount paid by codebtor.)

(c) Has either of you made any payments on the debts? (If so, specify total amount paid to each creditor, whether paid by husband or wife, and name of codebtor.)

14. Property and Exemptions (To be answered by debtor, if unmarried, otherwise for each spouse whether single or joint petition is filed.)

(a) *Real Property.*—List all real property owned by either of you at date of filing of original petition herein. (Indicate in last column whether owned solely by husband of wife, or jointly.)

Description and location of property	Name of any co-owner other than spouse	Present market value (without deduction for mortgage or other security interest)	Amount of mortgage or other security interest on this property	Name of mortgage or other secured creditor	Value claimed exempt. (Specify federal or state statute creating the exemption)	Owned solely by husband or wife, or jointly

(b) Personal Property.—List all other property owned by either of you at date of filing of original petition herein.

Description	Location of property if not at debtor's residence	Name of any co-owner other than spouse	Present market value (without deduction for mortgage or other security interest)	Amount of mortgage or other security interest on this property	Name of mortgage of other secured creditor	Value claimed exempt. (Specify federal or state statute creating the exemption)	Owned solely by husband or wife, or jointly
Auto (give year and make):							
Household goods:							
Personal effects:							
Cash or financial account:							
Other (specify):							

Unsworn Declaration under Penalty of Perjury
(To be signed by both spouses when joint petition is filed.)

I (*We*) _____ and _____
declare under penalty of perjury under the laws of the United States that I (*we*) have read the answers contained in the foregoing statement,
consisting of _____ sheets, and that they are true and complete to the best of my (*our*) knowledge, information, and belief.

Executed on _____ 19____ _____   _____
                                         Signature Husband (or Debtor)   Signature (Wife)

Attorney for Debtors & Address _____

_____

UNITED STATES BANKRUPTCY COURT FOR THE   DISTRICT OF   *Case No.*

In re
                                                                    } CHAPTER 13
                                                                      PLAN
Debtor, Soc. Sec. No.
[Include here all names used by debtor within last 6 years.]

(If this form is used by joint debtors wherever the word "debtor" or words referring to debtor are used they shall be read as if in the plural.)

1. The future earnings of the debtor are submitted to the supervision and control of the trustee and the [*debtor — debtor's employer*] shall pay
to the trustee the sum of $ *weekly — bi-weekly — semi-monthly — monthly.*

2. From the payments so received, the trustee shall make disbursements as follows:

    (a)   The priority payments required by 11 U.S.C. §507.

    (b)   After the above payments, dividends to secured creditors whose claims are duly proved and allowed as follows:

    (c)   *Subsequent to — pro rata with* dividends to secured creditors, dividends to unsecured creditors whose claims are duly proved and
            allowed as follows:

3. The following executory contracts of the debtor are rejected:

        Title to the debtor's property shall revest in the debtor *on confirmation of a plan — upon dismissal of the case after confirmation pursuant
to 11 U.S.C. §1329 — upon closing of the case pursuant to 11 U.S.C. §350.*

Dated:
                          _____   _____
                                    Debtor   *Debtor*

Acceptances may be mailed to _____   _____
                                                                  Post Office Address

BANKRUPT NAME & ADDRESS	ATTORNEY(S) NAME & ADDRESS	BANKRUPT/DEBTOR NO.
DISTRICT DIRECTOR INTERNAL REVENUE SERVICE DISTRICT OFFICE ADDRESS	START A-Z LIST OF CREDITORS	

DO NOT TYPE IN THIS AREA

If a debt is disclosed to the United States other than one for taxes, type an address for the United States Attorney for the district in which the case is pending and to the department, agent or instrumentality of the United States through which the bankrupt became indebted.

Check with your local district for addresses of state or local government agencies to which addressed label must be prepared.

UNITED STATES BANKRUPTCY COURT FOR THE   DISTRICT OF _____   Case No. _____

In re _____

                                                                      SCHEDULE OF
                                                                  }   CURRENT INCOME AND
                                                          Debtor*   CURRENT
                                                                      EXPENDITURES
Soc. Sec. No. _____ Debtor's Employer's Tax Id. No. _____

If this form is used by joint debtors wherever the question requires separate answers for Husband (H), Wife (W) or Joint (J) insert the appropriate symbol in column headed H, W or J.

Current Income

A. Give your current monthly income if unmarried, otherwise for each spouse whether single or joint petition is filed, unless spouses are separated and a single petition is filed.

                                                                         H, W or J
   (1) Debtor's monthly take-home pay _____   ____ $_____
   (2) Spouse's monthly take-home pay _____   ____ $_____
   (3) Regular income available from operation of a business or profession _____   ____ $_____
   (4) Do you receive alimony, maintenance or support payments?
      If so, state monthly amount _____   ____ $_____
      State the name, age and relationship to you of persons for whose benefit payments are received

      _____
      _____
      _____

   (5) Pension, social security or retirement income _____   ____ $_____

   (6) Other monthly income (specify) _____   ____ $_____
      _____   ____ $_____
      _____   ____ $_____
      _____   ____ $_____
      _____   ____ $_____
      _____   ____ $_____
      _____   Total $_____

Current Expenditures

B. Give current monthly expenditures of family, consisting of: H, W or J
   (1) Rent or home mortgage payment (include lot rental for trailer)_____   ____ $_____
   (2) (Electricity $_____   Heat $_____   Water $_____   Telephone $_____)   ____ $_____
   (3) Food _____   ____ $_____
   (4) Clothing _____   ____ $_____
   (5) Laundry and cleaning _____   ____ $_____
   (6) Newspapers, periodicals, and books (including school books) _____   ____ $_____
   (7) Medical and drug expenses _____   ____ $_____
   (8) Insurance (not deducted from wages): (a) Auto $_____ (b) Other $_____   ____ $_____
   (9) Transportation _____   ____ $_____
  (10) Recreation _____   ____ $_____
  (11) Dues, union, professional, social or otherwise (not deducted from wages)_____   ____ $_____
  (12) Taxes (not deducted from wages) _____   ____ $_____
  (13) Alimony, maintenance, or support payments _____   ____ $_____
      State the name, age and relationship to you of persons for whose benefit payments are made

      _____
      _____
      _____

  (14) Other payments for support of dependents not living at home _____   ____ $_____
  (15) Expenditures deducted from wages (specify) _____   ____ $_____
      _____   ____ $_____
      _____   ____ $_____
      _____   ____ $_____
      _____   ____ $_____
  (16) Other (specify) _____   ____ $_____
      _____   ____ $_____
      _____   ____ $_____
      _____   ____ $_____
      _____   ____ $_____
      _____   Total $_____

*Set forth here all names including tradenames used by Debtor within last 6 years.

Retirement, Income, Homestead and Other Exemption Protection

6

Most people concerned with asset protection—especially those who have incurred significant debts—are unaware that federal and state laws have been enacted to protect two of their most significant assets. Generally, an individual's retirement plan and home represent the primary portion of his or her wealth. The protections granted by law create specific exemptions for not just these two segments of your personal wealth, but also for your insurance, wages and other forms of income. This chapter will examine these specific exemptions.

Retirement and Pension Plans

Retirement and pension plans should be analyzed from the aspect of "qualified pension plans" and all other retirement plans, i.e., Individual Retirement Accounts, Governmental Pensions, and Individual Retirement Annuities.

"Qualified Retirement Plans" (the private pension system) is governed by the Employee Retirement Income Security Act of 1974 (ERISA). In order to be a qualified pension plan, a retirement plan must satisfy all of the provisions of ERISA, which was enacted to specifically protect the retirement funds of employees. A key ERISA requirement states that the plan must be a spendthrift trust if it is to qualify. Under the federal law, a spendthrift trust is one that prohibits its beneficiary from pledging or in any way "alienating" the principal or income of the plan.

If a plan qualifies, neither its income nor principal can be reached by the beneficiary's creditors. Section 401(a)(13) of the Internal Revenue Code requires that benefits of a plan may not be subject to garnishment or execution. This rule is subject to two major exceptions: (1) the prohibitions against attachment do not prevent the Internal Revenue Service from collecting federal tax liabilities from the plan, and (2) parties to a divorce action may attach benefits through a "Qualified Domestic Relations Order" (QDRO).

Further, the provisions of ERISA were written broadly so as to limit the ability of a state court, other than by way of a QDRO, to order payments to creditors from a pension plan.

This limitation on state courts was recently attacked successfully in one state court. That court breached the anti-alienation protection of ERISA by finding that the pension trust was not a spendthrift trust, as required by law. In order to find that the plan permitted its beneficiary to alienate his interest, the state court relied on state law principles. It pointed to the facts that the beneficiary in question was the (1) sole shareholder of the corporation that established the plan, (2) the only trustee of the plan, and (3) the sole beneficiary of the plan. Under state law (but not federal law), these facts would support a finding that the plan was not a spendthrift plan.

There is one other situation in which a qualified plan's beneficiary's interest may be reached by a creditor. Federal and state courts have also recognized an exemption to the anti-alienation rule based on an employee's fraud or criminal conduct against his or her employer. Again, this exemption has been very narrowly recognized, and when it is applied, only the employer can attack the beneficiary's interest in the plan.

Tip:

> *Are you the sole trustee of a pension plan in which you are the sole beneficiary? Many states have held that a plan trust cannot exist if the beneficiary is the sole trustee of the plan. It is highly advisable to name more than one trustee. Similarly, a husband and wife co-trustee situation may be subject to attack in the state court. Choose an independent person to serve as your co-trustee.*

Tip:

> *Do you use the pension monies as your private bank account? Plan*

> *loans to only the owner of a business will invite scrutiny. DO NOT GO TO THE PLAN LIKE A SAVINGS ACCOUNT. Monies deposited are intended for retirement.*

Tip:

> *Do not be afraid to allow your plan to accumulate large amounts of money. Some creditors' attorneys have argued that creditors should be allowed to reach unreasonable accumulations. To date, this argument has fallen on deaf ears.*

Bankruptcy

The Bankruptcy Courts have created a conflict regarding the treatment of qualified retirement plans. ERISA supersedes "any and all state laws insofar as they may relate now or hereafter to any employee benefit plan" [ERISA Section 206(d)]. However, since 1982, most bankruptcy courts have determined that the interest an individual has in a pension plan is subject to the jurisdiction of the court as property of the bankrupt estate. This approach was uniformly followed until 1990 when two courts swung the pendulum and exempted pension benefits from the bankrupt's estate.

Tip:

> *If you are a participant in a pension plan who has been forced to file for bankruptcy protection, list your pension plan interest but claim it as an exempt asset. At a minimum this places the burden on creditors to demonstrate that the pension is not exempt, and with the current swing you may succeed.*

Keogh Plans

If you are a participant in a Keogh plan that has multiple participants, the same principles that apply to qualified pension plans will apply to your Keogh plan. The plan is exempt from attachment by creditors generally and may even be exempt from creditors in bankruptcy.

A problem does arise in one-participant Keogh plans. These plans are not granted the same level of protection under ERISA. Many state courts have allowed attachment by creditors because (1) the funds may be withdrawn at will, and (2) an individual cannot be the trustee of a spendthrift trust for his or her benefit.

Tip:

> *If faced with this situation, look for a "friendly" co-trustee. The likelihood of a successful attack is greatly reduced when an "independent" trustee is responsible for the administration of the Plan and Trust. In this situation, it is probably safe to have your spouse serve as the co-trustee.*

IRAs

There is no federal protection for IRAs. They are by their nature custodial accounts that are set aside for retirement. They do not have a separate trustee. However, many state statutes exempt all retirement funds from attachment. There is a case in Pennsylvania where a bank attached an IRA it held in order to pay off a defaulted loan. The court emphatically denied the bank the monies, stating that retirement funds were not to be touched.

Tip:

> *Check your state's laws. If your particular state does not grant sanctuary to your retirement monies, consider transferring your IRA to a financial institution in a state that does protect such funds.*

Social Security

Notwithstanding the fact that Social Security is not a pension for purposes of ERISA, Social Security payments of all types, including disability payments, are fully exempt from attachment by creditors.

Homestead Protection

Most states protect family homes from attachment by creditors. The "homestead exemption" provides protection for what is probably the most significant asset owned by most families. Under the exemption, the homeowner or family head is permitted to exempt the homestead from execution for general debts. Obviously, the exemption does not protect the property from mortgage foreclosure actions.

What Is a Homestead?

A "homestead" is the primary residence of the head of the family. The exemption is limited to one property. The residence, however, need not be a single-family home—it can be an apartment, a condominium or even undeveloped land.

Your state's statutes will provide the technical requirements for electing the exemption. It is clear, however, that the exemption attaches only to the primary residence. You, therefore, must carefully choose which property to protect if you have more than one "homestead." A vacation home, for example, may have greater value than your "primary residence." If you own more than one home, therefore, do not automatically assume that the dwelling place you use for the better part of the year should be categorized as your "homestead."

Who Can Elect?

Generally, only one spouse can exercise the homestead exemption. For this reason, careful consideration should be given to the question of who should be deemed the head of the family for purposes of the exemption. The wisest course is to determine which spouse is most vulnerable to attack from creditors and to designate that person the head of the household. In many families today both spouses may be "breadwinners," and there may not be a clear-cut answer to the question of which spouse is more vulnerable. One guideline that may help two-earner families resolve this question calls for the spouse who is self-employed to be deemed the head of the family. This approach recognizes the fact that a self-employed person usually runs greater financial risks than an employee.

Which Debts Are Exempt?

State law usually determines the precise nature of debts against which the homestead exemption applies and those against which it does not provide a shield. There are only two categories of debt to consider: (1) those you incurred before you purchased the property for which you seek the exemption, and (2) debts incurred after you purchased the property for which you seek the exemption.

Virtually every state will allow its exemption to shield the property from debts incurred after the purchase of the family home. The states are split, however, on how to apply the exemption with respect to debts incurred before the purchase of a home. Some states permit the exemption to protect the family home regardless of when the debt was incurred; others take a more restrictive position and do not enforce the exemption against debts incurred before the purchase of the family home.

How Much Protection Is Available?

Every state has its own rules governing the amount of the homestead exemption. In a few states, New Jersey, for example, your home is entirely unprotected. At the other extreme are states, Florida, for example, that shield your home against all debts (other than IRS debts), whatever their size and whenever they were incurred. Recent articles, in fact, have reported that large-wealth individuals have purchased multimillion dollar homes in Florida in order to take advantage of its generous homestead exemption.

Factors to Consider

Ultimately, the election of the homestead exemption may not provide you with sufficient protection from creditors nor may it offer sufficient protection for your home itself. Despite the fact that it is not an all-in-one answer to asset protection needs, the exemption does provide you with a valuable tool in your overall efforts to build a complete asset protection structure to shelter yourself and your family from attacks by creditors. When you review the homestead exemption as you build your asset protection program, you should consider the following potential problems:

(1)   If your state's homestead exemption law does not exempt the entire value of your home from attack by creditors, then a significant portion of your equity (the difference between your home's fair market value and the mortgage(s) on your home) may be exposed to risk.

(2)   Even in states that allow the exemption to protect all of your equity in your home, the homestead exemption will not protect your home from attack by mortgagees or the Internal Revenue Service.

(3)   In some states, the exemption may not protect your home against claims from creditors on debts that you incurred before you purchased your home.

(4)   Should you decide to sell or refinance your home after electing to exercise your homestead exemption, you may run into legal tangles. Although these tangles can be unknotted, it may take additional time to close on the refinancing or sale.

Tip:

> *Given the financial and emotional significance of the asset in question—your home—you should consult an attorney familiar with your state's law to find out (1) whether the homestead ex-* *emption applies to all debts, regardless of when they were incurred, (2) the amount of the exemption and (3) what you must do to insure that you do not lose this potentially vital form of protection.*

Life Insurance

Life insurance, in today's society, can address many needs: protection for one's spouse or children, investment options and income stream needs. When the first exemptions for life insurance were drafted, the state legislatures were concerned primarily with protecting the family of the insured. Today, all fifty states grant an exemption for life insurance whether it is purchased by the insured person individually or as part of a group plan.

Where the states differ is in the amount of the exemption. Many states exempt all of the proceeds of the policy (as well as the cash surrender value of whole life polices) from creditors' claims. If a state's exemption provision is limited to a specific dollar amount, then any amount above that limit is available to satisfy claims made by creditors of the insured. Similarly, the state exemption provisions may cover the cash surrender value of whole life policies. If, however, the state sets a limit on the amount of the exemption, then amounts above the limit on the cash surrender value of the policy may be reached by creditors.

The exemption also applies if the life insurance policy is investment sensitive. Given the various new techniques adopted by insurance companies to make life insurance an investment technique that is designed to provide an income stream for the insured, it is possible that such policies may come under attack from creditors of the insured in the future. As of now, no state court appears to have denied the exemption to life insurance policies that have a substantial investment motive, and you may want to consider the use of life insurance as part of your overall planning to protect your assets.

Maximizing Your Protection

In order to gain maximum protection from the exemption offered for life insurance, there are several factors you should consider and act upon:

(1)   If you are the beneficiary of a policy, some states will extend the exemption to you with respect to either all or a portion of the proceeds. In those states that offer no such exemption or only limited protection, your creditors may be able to reach all or part of the proceeds.

(2)   Even in states that extend the exemption to beneficiaries, you must be careful not to mingle insurance proceeds with other funds. If you permit commingling, you run the risk of losing the exemption.

(3)   If your home state does not extend the exemption to beneficiaries, you may want to ask the insured person (or the owner of the policy if the owner is not the insured person) to create a trust and name it as the beneficiary of the policy and you as a beneficiary of the trust. Another option is to ask to have your spouse or children named as the beneficiaries of the policy.

(4)   If you want to maximize the protection of both the cash surrender value portion of your policy and the proceeds of the policy, consider creating an irrevocable life insurance trust. This step may also provide you with additional tax benefits.

Welfare Payments

Because they are offered to enable people in need to live at a subsistence level, aid to families with dependent children is granted an exemption from garnishment by at least half of the states in the country. Several states extend this exemption to other public assistance payments, such as those made to the blind, the disabled and the elderly. By the same token, nearly half of all of the states do not offer any exemption protection for public assistance funds.

In states where the exemption exists, most laws are worded so that the state cannot be garnished for payments to be made to recipients. In those states the exemptions also remain in place after the money is paid to the recipient. But, to ensure that creditors do not reach the payment after it has been made, the recipient should take care not to commingle public assistance payments with other monies they may have, since creditors may be able to reach a commingled fund.

Wages, Alimony, Child Support

Most states have taken the position that it is in the best interests of the public to exempt employees' wages from attachment by creditors. Some states go so far as to completely bar the attachment and garnishment of wages, e.g., Florida, Pennsylvania and Texas. But, even in those states the protection against attachment and garnishment does not extend to either child support or alimony payments that a court has ordered.

Even if your state offers only limited protection against garnishment, there is a federal law that may protect your wages. The Consumer Credit Protection Act, a federal law, sets a maximum on the amount that can be garnished from your wages. The federal limit looks to the garnishee's disposable income, i.e., the amount left in your paycheck after federal and state withholding taxes and payments have been taken out. That limit is the lesser of (1) 25 percent of the garnishee's disposable income or (2) the amount by which the garnishee's disposable income exceeds 30 times the existing hourly federal minimum wage rate. Like the state provisions, the Consumer Credit Protection Act does not apply to garnishments sought for child support or alimony payments ordered by a court.

Set out below is a listing of the income exemptions provided by each state.

STATE HOMESTEAD AND INCOME EXEMPTIONS

State	Homestead Exemption	Amount Subject to Garnishments
Alabama	$5000, not to exceed 160 acres of land. Alabama Con. 6-10-2.	25% of wages. Alabama Con. 6-10-7.
Alaska	$54,000. Alaska Stat. 9.38.010	Wages in excess of $350 per week. Alaska Stat. 9.38.030.
Arizona	$100,000, including traceable cash proceeds for 18 months after sale. Arizona Stat. 33-1101.	Lesser of amount in excess of 30 times federal minimum wage or 25% of earnings. Arizona Stat. 33-1131.
Arkansas	$2,500, but if outside of town at least 160 acres and at least 1/4 acre inside of town. Arkansas Stat. 16-66-210.	Earnings in excess of $25 per week for 60 days. Arkansas Stat. 16-66-208.
California	$75,000, increases to $100,000 if 65 or older or over 55 and disabled. California Cons. 704.730.	No exemption.
Colorado	$20,000 if owner occupied, including traceable proceeds for one year. Colorado Stats. 38-41-201.	Lesser of excess of 30 times federal minimum wage or 25% of earnings. Colorado Stat. 5-5-105.
Connecticut	None.	Greater of excess of 40 times federal minimum wage or 25% of earnings. Connecticut Stat. 52-361.
Delaware	None.	15% of wages. 10 Delaware Code Annot. § 4913.
Florida	150 contiguous acres outside municipality or 1/2 acre inside municipality.	0%. Florida Stat. Annot. 222.11.

Georgia	$5,000. Georgia Cons. Laws Annot. 44-13-1.	Lesser of excess of 30 times federal minimum wage or 25%. Georgia Cons. Laws Annot. 18-4-20.
Hawaii	$20,000; increased to $30,000 if over age 65 or head of household. Hawaii Stat. 651-92.	0%. Hawaii Stat. 651-121.
Idaho	$30,000. Idaho Cons. Laws 55-1003.	Lesser of excess of 30 times federal minimum wage or 25%. Idaho Cons. Laws 11-207.
Illinois	$7,500, including traceable proceeds for one year. Illinois Stat. Annot. 12-901.	Lesser of excess of 40 times federal minimum wage or 15% of gross earnings. Illinois Stat. Annot. 12-803.
Indiana	$7,500. Indiana Stat. 34-2-28-1.	Lesser of excess of 30 times federal minimum wage or 25% of earnings. Indiana Stat. 24-4.5-5-105.
Iowa	40 acres if not within city; 1/2 acre if within city; both at least $500 in value. Iowa Code 561-2.	Lesser of excess of 40 times federal minimum wage or 25% of earnings limited to no more than 10% of earnings. Iowa Code 642-21.
Kansas	160 acres of rural land; 1 acre in city. Kansas Stat. Annot. 60-2301.	Lesser of excess of 30 times federal minimum wage or 25% of earnings. Kansas Stat. Annot. 60-2310.
Kentucky	$5,000. Kentucky Stat. 427.060.	Lesser of excess of 30 times federal minimum wage or 25% of earnings. Kentucky Stat. 427.010.

Louisiana	160 acres, not to exceed $15,000 in value. Louisiana Stat. Annot. 20:1.	Greater of excess of 30 times federal minimum wage or 25% of earnings. Louisiana Stat. Annot. 13:3881A.
Maine	$7,500, increasing to $60,000 if over age 60 or disabled, with disabled dependent. Maine Stat. Annot. 4422.	100%.
Maryland	Only bankruptcy, then $2,500. Maryland Stat. 11-504.	Lesser of amount in excess of $145 per week or 25% of earnings. Maryland Stat. 15-601.1.
Massachusetts	$100,000 but must be declared. Massachusetts Laws Annot. 188 § 1.	Lesser of 25% of earnings or amount in excess of $10. Massachusetts Law Annot. 154 § 2.
Michigan	$3,500, not to exceed 40 acres if rural or one lot in city. Michigan Stat. Annot. 27A.6023.	100%.
Minnesota	160 acres if outside city; 1/2 acre if in city. Minnesota Stat. 510.01.	Lesser of excess of 40 times federal minimum wage or 25% of earnings. Minnesota Stat. 571.55.
Mississippi	160 acres not to exceed $30,000 in value. Mississippi Cons. Annot. 85-3-21.	0% for 30 days then lesser of excess of 30 times federal minimum wage or 25% of earnings. Mississippi Cons. Annot. 85-3-4.
Missouri	None.	Lesser of excess of 30 times federal minimum wage or 25% of earnings. (10% if head of house). Missouri Stat. 525.030.
Montana	$40,000 including traceable proceeds for 18 months. Montana Cons. Annot. 70-32-104.	Lesser of excess of 30 times federal minimum wage or 25% of earnings. Montana Const. Annot. 25-13-614.

Nebraska	160 acres if outside city; 1/2 acre in city, not to exceed $10,000 in value. Nebraska Stat. 1943 § 40-101.	Lesser of excess of 30 times federal minimum wage or 25% (15% head of house) of earnings. Nebraska Stat. 1943 § 25-1558.
Nevada	$95,000; must declare in writing. Nevada Stat. 115.01.	Lesser of excess of 30 times federal minimum wage or 25% of earnings. Nevada Stat. 21.090.
New Hampshire	$5,000. New Hampshire Rev. Stat. Annot. § 480:1.	100%.
New Jersey	None.	100% over $7,500 per year; 10% if more than $48 per week and $7,500 for year; 0% if earnings less than $48 per week. New Jersey Stat. Annot. 2A:17-50.
New Mexico	$20,000. New Mexico Stat. 42-10-9.	Lesser of excess of 40 times federal minimum wage or 25% of earnings. New Mexico Stat. 35-12-7.
New York	$10,000. New York Civ. Prac. Law 5206.	100%.
North Carolina	$7,500, offset by personal claims. North Carolina Stat. 1C-1601.	60 days of wages. North Carolina Stat. 1-362.
North Dakota	$80,000, including proceeds from sale. North Dakota Cons. 47-18-1.	Lesser of excess of 40 times federal minimum wage or 25% of earnings. North Dakota Cons. 28-22-2.
Ohio	$5,000, offset by personal claim. Ohio Rev. Code 2329.66.	Lesser of excess of 30 times federal minimum wage or 25% of earnings. Ohio Rev. Code 2329.66.

Oklahoma	160 acres if outside city; 1 acre if inside city; not to exceed $5,000 in value. Oklahoma Stat. Annot. 1A1.	25%. Oklahoma Stat. Annot. 1A18.
Oregon	60 acres outside city; 1 block in city, not to exceed $15,000 in value. Oregon Rev. Stat. 23.240.	Lesser of excess of 40 times federal minimum wage or 25% of earnings. Oregon Rev. Stat. 23.185.
Pennsylvania	None.	0%. Pennsylvania Cons. Stat. 8127.
Rhode Island	None	Wages in excess of $50 per week. Rhode Island Laws 9-26-4.
South Carolina	$5,000, offset by personal claims. South Carolina Cons. Stat. 15-41-30.	0%. South Carolina Cons. Stat. 15-39-410.
South Dakota	100% protected. South Dakota Cons. Laws 43-31-1.	0% for 60 days. South Dakota Cons. Laws 15-20-12.
Tennessee	$5,000 ($7,500 jointly). Tennessee Cons. Annot. 26-2-30.	Lesser of excess of 30 times federal minimum wage or 25% of earnings. Tennessee Cons. Annot. 26-2-106.
Texas	100 acres (200 for family) outside city; 1 acre in city. Texas Prop. Code 41.001.	0%. Texas Annot. Rev. Stat. 4099.
Utah	$8,000 for head of house, includes traceable proceeds for one year. Utah Cons. Annot. 78-23-3.	100%.
Vermont	$30,000. Vermont Stat. Annot. 101.	Lesser of excess of 30 times federal minimum wage or 25% of earnings. Vermont Stat. Annot. 3170.

Virginia	$5,000 offset by personal exemption claim. Virginia Stat. 34-4.	Lesser of excess of 30 times federal minimum wage or 25% of earnings. Virginia Stat. 34-29.
Washington	$30,000, including traceable proceeds for one year. Washington Stat. 6.12.010.	Lesser of excess of 30 times federal minimum wage or 25% of earnings. Washington Stat. 7.33.280.
West Virginia	$5,000 for head of house. West Virginia Cons. 38-9-1.	100%.
Wisconsin	$40,000, including traceable proceeds for 2 years if intent to purchase new homestead. Wisconsin Stat. Annot. 815.21.	Lesser of excess of 30 times federal minimum wage or 25% of earnings. Wisconsin Stat. Annot. 815.18.
Wyoming	$10,000, must be owner occupied. Wyoming Stat. Annot. 1-20-101.	50% of earnings. Wyoming Stat. Annot. 1-17-411.
District of Columbia	None.	Lesser of excess of 30 times federal minimum wage or 25% of earnings. District of Columbia Civ. 16-572.

Using Trusts and Joint Tenancies to Protect Your Assets

7

The form under which property is owned plays a vital role in any asset protection program. Essentially, you may hold property in your own name (or jointly with another person) or you may choose to put the property into a trust. Depending upon how you structure the ownership, both individual ownership and the trust can protect many of your personal assets.

Trusts

There are two primary purposes for creating a trust:

1. Tax planning and savings for estates, and

2. Maintaining privacy with respect to your personal finances and transactions.

Both of these needs can be satisfied by a trust. A properly written "spendthrift" trust bars creditors from reaching the assets placed in the trust. The spendthrift trust, therefore, protects the property against the claims of two sets of creditors—those of the person who establishes the trust as well as those of the trust's beneficiary.

In addition to asset protection, a trust provides a family with the ability to (1) transfer wealth from parent to child, (2) reduce the costs of probate, and (3) provide an independent trustee to manage the finances of individuals who may not be able to take care of themselves. It is beyond the scope of this book to examine the tax advantages of trusts, but before creating a trust you must look into the tax concerns.

In essence, there are two types of trusts: Revocable and Irrevocable. The level of asset protection depends on the (1) type of trust chosen, (2) powers you retain, and (3) term or life of the trust. Trusts can be established during your life or by your will.

Irrevocable Trust

The term "irrevocable" means that once the trust is established you no longer have the right or authority to change or alter the terms of the trust. There is one exception to this rule: most state laws will allow you to nominate successor trustees without breaking the irrevocability of the trust.

The irrevocable trust is the most potent trust vehicle for asset protection. The strength of this strategy stems from the fact that you have completely and irrevocably transferred ownership of the property to another. In effect, you have gifted the property away. The property is shielded from your creditors because you no longer own it and you will not be getting the property back in the future. As always, you must be careful that the transfer to the trust is not considered a fraudulent conveyance. If so, your creditors may be able to break the protections of the trust.

You cannot be both the grantor (the person setting up the trust) and the beneficiary (the person who receives income and/or the principal of the trust). Most states do not recognize spendthrift trusts if the person who sets up the trust and the beneficiary is the same individual. This is considered a fraudulent transfer on its face.

How do you set up an Irrevocable Trust? It is critically important for accomplishing asset protection that the trust be carefully written and that all irrevocable trust criteria be satisfied completely. The most important decision you will make is identifying the Trustee. You should not be the trustee. You do not want to give even the least impression that you are still the owner of the property, and under trust law the Trustee is the "legal title owner" of the property in the trust.

Who is to be the beneficiary? The beneficiary is the person who ultimately receives or benefits from the property. It can be anyone, but most likely the beneficiary will be your spouse or children, or other family members if you are not married. What the trust accomplishes is to delay the outright transfer of the trust property to the beneficiary until some established future time or event. The trust document defines that future time or event. The time can be measured in years, e.g., ten years from the establishment of the trust. An event can be a predetermined occurrence such as someone retiring from work or death.

The Irrevocable Minor's Trust

The Tax Reform Act of 1986 gutted the tax benefits that had been available from Minor's Trusts. The ability to "split income" between a parent and child, taking advantage of the child's lower income bracket, has been removed for children under age 14. However, in the asset protection realm the Minor's Trust is still a valuable tool.

A Minor's Trust is a vehicle that enables parents to make gifts of property to their children and ensure that the property is protected until the child is "mature" enough not to waste the gift. Further, the use of the trust places the property in the hands of a
Trustee, thereby allowing the property to be disposed of properly even while the child is a minor. Remember, a minor is allowed to disavow contracts entered into prior to their reaching the age of majority.

The Minor's Trust is governed by two subsections of the Internal Revenue Code— Section 2503(b) and (c). Both subsections set the age of majority at 21, regardless of your state's law. The benefit of a Minor's Trust is that your creditors cannot reach the assets transferred into the trust, nor can your child's creditors reach the assets while they are in the trust.

Section 2503(c) Minor's Trusts

A 2503(c) Minor's Trust requires the trust to distribute any retained principal and income that has not been paid for the benefit of the beneficiary on his or her 21st birthday. Further, it requires that should the minor die prior to reaching age 21, his or her interest must be paid to the child's estate.

The law allows a 2503(c) Minor's Trust to continue past the individual's 21st birthday, but only if no restrictions bar the beneficiary from getting the trust property at any point in time after turning 21.

This trust blocks creditors from reaching property that you intend to use to take care of your children. It can also protect, during your child's minority, property from your children's creditors. It cannot, however, stop your children's creditors from reaching the property after your children turn 21.

Section 2503(b) Minor's Trusts

A better alternative might be the 2503(b) Minor's Trust. In a sense the term "Minor's Trust" is a misnomer, because the trust can last beyond a person's minority. It can last even as long as the beneficiary's entire life. Another difference between the 2503(b) and (c) Minor's Trusts is that the 2503(b) Minor's Trust must distribute the income it earns at least once a year. However, the principal of the trust does not have to be distributed to the income beneficiary. That is, you can have income payable to your child for life, and upon the child's death, the principal can be paid to his or her children.

The Section 2503(b) trust provides limited protection from creditors. Creditors cannot reach the principal of the trust, but the income—if distributed directly to your child—may be attached by their creditors.

TRAP: Both forms of Minor's Trust can have income tax ramifications for both you and your child. If your child is under age 14, the income that is distributed to him or for his benefit will be taxed at your personal rate. Any income that is retained in the 2503(c) trust will be taxed at trust tax rates, which are generally higher than individual tax rates. Finally, if the trust is used to pay for support obligations, the parents would have income, too, since they have been relieved of that obligation.

Life Insurance Trusts

Life insurance, in today's market, is more than "just insurance." It is an asset. Many insurance policies are designed to provide income or an investment that will grow tax free. As such, insurance is an asset that may be attacked by your creditors.

Keep in mind that, in the business loan setting, most lenders will require the assignment of insurance as additional collateral for loans. If your insurance is to be used to provide for the care of your family, it is imperative that you plan to insulate the insurance from your creditors.

The procedure used to establish a life insurance trust is similar to that used to establish trusts generally. It requires a written document, a trustee, a beneficiary, and terms of distribution. Generally, life insurance trusts are established with more concern for tax savings than asset protection.

However, as noted, some insurance policies can accumulate significant value other than as a death benefit.

The life insurance trust can be revocable or irrevocable. The irrevocable insurance trust provides the greatest asset protection. The trust can be "unfunded"—this means that the only asset the trust owns is the insurance policy on your life. Such a trust is considered unfunded because the insurance contract is a promise to pay later and, for that reason, does not become a tangible asset until the insured's death.

Insurance can also be placed in a revocable or living trust. As an asset protection strategy, this provides little protection. As will be discussed, the grantor (the individual who establishes the trust) is treated as the owner of property in a revocable trust since that individual has the ability, by the terms

Insiders' Guide to Complete Asset Protection

of the trust, to terminate the trust at any time. The revocable insurance trust is more properly an estate tax device than an asset protection tool.

Revocable Trusts

Revocable trusts get their name from their nature. You can revoke it at any time during your life. Not until your death does a revocable trust become irrevocable. It becomes irrevocable at your death since you are the only person who can alter, amend or terminate the trust. Upon your death, therefore, no one has the power to subsequently change the trust—at least without court approval—and it becomes irrevocable.

Revocable trusts offer no asset protection if the trust is for your benefit during your life. Some states may concede that the trust is a separate legal entity and is not responsible for your debts. The general rule, however, is that a person cannot be his own trustee and, therefore, the trust's assets are reachable by creditors.

What if you have an independent trustee.? In that situation, state laws vary. You may successfully exempt some property from creditors by virtue of your not having ownership over the property.

As with many of the techniques we've discussed, a revocable trust does not grant immunity, but it may dissuade a less than enthusiastic creditor from pursuing your property. If your debt is not sufficient to justify the legal expenses involved, your creditor may not be willing to sue to (1) reduce his claim to judgment, and (2) force you to revoke your revocable trust and turn over the proceeds.

The strongest protection offered by a revocable trust comes into existence when the grantor dies. At that point, the trust becomes irrevocable, and the beneficiaries will receive the property according to the terms of the trust.

When the grantor dies, the grantor's creditors may be out of luck. If funded prior to his death, the revocable trust need not pay creditors out of trust estate unless there has been a fraudulent transfer.

The Foreign-Based Trust

The foreign-based trust is perhaps the newest asset protection program to have been developed. It is easily the safest form of asset protection available today. Designed primarily for professionals who fear outlandish judgments in malpractice litigation and business people who are concerned with extensive liability flowing from deals that go bad, the foreign-based trust overcomes all of the drawbacks of every other trust form.

The benefits of the foreign-based trust are remarkable. First, it protects the principal from attacks by creditors, even in situations that could be termed fraudulent under U.S. law. Second, it allows the grantor to receive income from the trust and to maintain effective control over the ways in which the trust's principal is invested and distributed.

The foreign-based trust is established in much the same way any other trust is created. Under the terms of a written trust agreement, a grantor places assets in a trust, names a trustee, and identifies the beneficiary. The only difference between this form of trust and others we have discussed is that it is created under the laws of a friendly foreign jurisdiction such as the Isle of Mann or the Cook Islands. Should you be concerned that creating a trust in a foreign jurisdiction is a risky venture, you should be advised that the Isle of Mann is a British protectorate located several miles off the shores of Scotland and that the Cook Islands is a dependency of New Zealand. Both are stable, secure jurisdictions, and both have very favorable trust laws.

By setting up your foreign-based trust in a friendly jurisdiction, you will be gaining the advantages of laws that permit you to create an irrevocable trust in which you are the named beneficiary. Although you will have to name an independent trustee who is a resident of the foreign jurisdiction, you can replace the trustee at any time if he or she does not satisfy your standards. Further, the trust document can require the trustee to get your approval before making an investment or a distribution of assets. You, therefore, remain in control.

For the most part, these foreign jurisdictions prohibit creditors from reaching assets placed in an irrevocable trust. Where they differ from jurisdictions in this country is in the roadblocks they set before creditors who seek to pierce a trust on the grounds that the trust was created in a fraudulent manner. Those jurisdictions will not recognize a judgment from a court in this country to the effect that the grantor acted fraudulently. Instead, if the creditor wishes to make that claim, it must do so in the courts of the foreign jurisdiction and must prove its case

under the laws of that jurisdiction. So, for example, if a creditor wishes to enforce a judgment against you, he or she must go to the Cook Islands (about 1,800 miles northeast of New Zealand), sue you all over again, and prove the case against you all over again (but, this time under Cook Island law). Equally important, the Cook Island law takes a much different approach to defining a fraudulent transfer than do the laws of the states of this country. Obviously, they are more favorable to the debtor.

Foreign-based trusts, however, are not for everyone. First, they cannot be created on a do-it-yourself basis. You will need the assistance of a qualified lawyer, and the fees for such services run as high as $15,000. The annual fee for the trustee may range between $1,000 to $2,500 a year. Given those costs, the foreign-based trust probably is the tool of choice for individuals who are exposed to the risks of massive judgments. For those people, however, the foreign-based trust is—beyond any doubt—a virtually impregnable shield for asset protection purposes.

The Medicaid Trust

The Medicaid Trust was created to protect individuals from the cost of a catastrophic illness. It is a form of irrevocable trust that may have only limited value against business or personal creditors, but it is an invaluable tool should the person creating the trust fall victim to a catastrophic illness.

What the Medicaid Trust does is to ensure that the principal amount you place in the trust cannot be used by the state to disqualify you from Medicaid assistance. Medicaid assistance is limited to individuals who, for our purposes, have virtually no meaningful assets to their name.

A Medicaid Trust is formed in much the same way as other trusts; the grantor places assets in an irrevocable trust and names another person as the trustee. Unlike other types of irrevocable trusts, however, the grantor is named as the income beneficiary and either a spouse or children as the

beneficiaries of the trust's principal.

That means that the grantor will continue to enjoy the income of the trust's assets for the rest of his or her life. In the event the grantor should require extended or permanent nursing care, he or she will qualify for Medicare and will have the funds to supplement Medicare assistance in order to choose an appropriate nursing facility.

Because the income from the trust goes back to the grantor, creditors of the grantor can reach that money to satisfy their claims, and, in many states, may be able to reach the principal amount put into the trust.

The Medicare Trust is a special purpose trust. It is not designed to protect your assets from creditor attack. Instead, it is used to ensure that should a crippling illness arise, the principal that you worked a lifetime to create will not be lost to hospitals and nursing care centers. This trust enables you to qualify for Medicare, and, if necessary, to procure assistance at a higher level than Medicare will provide.

There are two practical matters you should keep in mind if you believe you probably do not need a Medicaid Trust. First, current research indicates that seven out of every ten people will be forced to consider the need for long-term medical care during their lifetime and that the cost of such care in a nursing home ranges between $25,000 and $50,000 a year. Second, you cannot expect to gain the benefits of a Medicaid Trust if you wait until disaster strikes. The state can go after any assets you have transferred into a Medicaid Trust unless the transfer was made 30 months before you enter a nursing home.

Business Trusts—Massachusetts Business Trusts (MBT)

Business trusts are more typically known as Massachusetts Business Trusts (MBT), since Massachusetts was the state that first recognized them. In essence, an MBT provides for the operation of property or a business in a trust format. The MBT grants the trust certificate holders limited liability, much like what a corporation is permitted to offer its shareholders. Many states, however, require some form of registration of the MBT. For federal tax purposes, an MBT is treated as a corporation. For these reasons, it may be just as easy and efficient to form a corporation as it is to start an MBT.

The primary advantage of an MBT over a corporation is that the affairs of the MBT are private. But in any contested litigation the privacy of the MBT does not become a privilege limiting a creditor's right to obtain information.

Many states require strict adherence to their statutes to obtain the limited liability benefit of an MBT. Failure to do so might result in your having personal liability for business obligations.

All things considered, the corporate form of a business is a safer vehicle for providing protection from business debts than an MBT.

Land Trusts

Some trust strategies provide only a false sense of security as an asset protector. This is particularly true in the case of a land trust. Created under state law, the land trust is a special form of revocable trust.

The primary benefit of a land trust is the privacy it provides for the trust owners. When a property is titled in the name of the land trust, creditors searching the recorder of deeds will only find the name of the trustee, not the true owners. This provides "protection" from reverse research, that is, finding the owner based on the property. It does not protect you from disclosing your interest if you are directly asked by a creditor, particularly if the inquiry comes when you are under oath.

As with many strategies adopted to protect assets from creditors, the more complicated the strategy the more complications that will arise regarding the disposition of assets. Although a trustee will not disclose to outsiders who the owners of the property are, the trustee may not want to accept liability for some transactions. The trustee may require you to dissolve the trust in order to sell the property.

In addition, a major drawback to a land trust is that your ownership in the trust is not considered ownership of the land for federal tax purposes. Instead you are deemed to own personal property, not real property. This will impact your ability to claim a homestead exemption (see Chapter 6) and your ability to transfer the land in a like-kind exchange under Internal Revenue Code

Section 1031. Further, dissolving the trust just to enter into a like-kind exchange may not result in the property qualifying for the tax free treatment.

Finally, the land trust may result in additional costs to you. Some states will re-quire the payment of transfer taxes on each transfer in and out of the trust to the beneficial owners. Check with your state's recorder of deeds office to find out if you must pay a transfer tax.

Bolstering the Asset Protection of a Trust

1. If possible, use an irrevocable trust. As discussed, you give away the property in an irrevocable trust so neither your creditors, nor your beneficiaries' creditors, can reach the property while the assets are held in trust.

2. Have a non-protection reason for establishing the trust. This is similar to having a "business purpose" for pursuing some transactions. Courts are loathe to pierce trusts as asset protectors if the trust has been established for estate planning purposes or to provide for the education of a family member.

3. Choose an "independent" trustee. You should not be the trustee. An outsider, no matter how friendly, must exercise his own fiduciary duty to the trust. If the trust limits or establishes objective guidelines on how the trustee can invest trust property, then the courts generally do not look beyond the terms of the trust.

Joint Ownership

The most common form of property ownership in the family situation is joint ownership, since it eases the eventual disposition of property. It allows more than one person to have access to and benefit from the property. So, for example, consider how many people have joint checking or savings accounts. This type of ownership is not limited to married people. To the contrary, many joint accounts are between parents and children, especially for elderly parents who may need the help of children in their daily financial affairs.

In this section we will briefly examine the different types of joint ownership and the difficulties they create for the judgment creditor.

Types of Co-Ownership

There are three types of co-ownership. Each co-tenancy creates specific legal rights, and state law determines how a creditor can attack the property when held in a joint title.

The three types of ownership are:

- Tenants in Common
- Joint Tenants
- Tenants by the Entirety

Tenants in Common

A tenants in common form of ownership creates an interest in the property which is divided among the co-owners. This allows each individual to sell or transfer his or her interest in the property without the consent of the other tenants.

This transferability feature exposes a tenant in common's interest in property to execution by his or her creditors. The creditor can either take the debtor's interest or request the court to sell the property or, in the case of securities or land, partition the property and then sell it.

Joint Tenant

The primary difference between joint tenancy and tenants in common is the fact that a joint tenancy creates an undivided interest in property. The joint tenancy can be either equal or unequal ownership interests, depending on the titling.

Joint tenancy generally must be established by a written document. In the case of real estate, the deed satisfies the need for a writing if it transfers the property to two or more individuals as joint tenants. Most states require some recitation that a joint tenancy has been created or they will treat the co-ownership as a tenants in common relationship.

The strength of joint tenancy in protecting assets lies in the fact that each tenant has an undivided interest. This undivided nature of ownership dissuades creditors in two ways: (1) the value of an undivided interest is less than that of a divided interest, and (2) the ability to cause a partition of the property is greatly reduced.

Further, joint tenancy grants the survivor of the joint tenants the property. It is similar to a winner-take-all pool. During the lives of the tenants, they can all agree to sell or end this form of ownership, but on death, the last to survive inherits all.

Tenants by the Entirety

A special form of joint tenants is tenants by the entirety. It may be established only by husbands and wives. The ownership of property in tenants by the entirety may only be transferred on the agreement of both husband and wife, and the survivor inherits the property on the death of the other. Of special importance is that tenants by the entirety property does not pass according to a will; instead, it passes by operation of law to the survivor.

The benefit of this form of ownership is that creditors cannot attach and sell the property unless both owners are party to the

debt. Accordingly, if one person has a large judgment or debt against him or her, the creditor cannot get the property if the other spouse is not a party to the debt. One caution: if the non-debtor spouse dies, the creditor can perfect his claim and take the property. Conversely, if the debtor dies first, the creditor cannot reach the property.

Several states have abolished the tenancy by the entirety concept, but about half of the states still recognize it. In some states, e.g., Pennsylvania, tenants by the entirety completely bars creditors from executing against joint property for individual debts.

IRREVOCABLE TRUST

TRUST AGREEMENT made the　　　　　day

of　　　　　　　, 19　　, by and between

(hereinafter referred to as the "Settlors") and

(hereinafter referred to as the "Trustee").

1. Property of Settlors. The Settlors transfer, assign, convey and quitclaim to the Trustee and to its successors in trust, the property described in Schedule "A", attached hereto, to have and to hold such property and any other property of any kind which the Trustee may, at any time, hereafter hold or acquire pursuant to any of the provisions hereof (all of which property is referred to hereinafter as the "Trust Estate"), subject to the trust, purposes, and conditions set forth.

2. Additional Property. Either of the Settlors or any other person shall have the right at any time, to transfer, assign and convey, deliver, devise and bequeath to the Trustee any additional cash, security, and other property in addition to the property presently transferred and delivered, or by having the proceeds of insurance policies made payable to the Trustee or by bequest or devise by will having proceeds payable to the Trustee and such cash, security, life insurance proceeds, and other property shall be held, administered, and disposed of by the Trustee as part of the trust estate in accordance with the provisions of this Trust Agreement without the execution of any further instrument or declaration.

3. Insurance Policies. The Settlors have caused or may cause the Trustee to be named as beneficiary of the insurance policies listed in the Schedule "B", attached hereto, and the Trustee accepts the designation in trust for the purposes and on the conditions set forth. The Settlors or any other person may at any time add any additional policy or policies of insurance to this Trust by assigning the policy or policies to the Trustee or by naming the Trustee as beneficiary. In either case, the policy and its proceeds shall be subject to the terms and conditions of this Agreement.

4. Trustee's Duties During the Lifetime of the Settlors. During the lifetime of the Settlors, the Trustee shall hold the Trust Fund for the following purposes:

    (a)   The Trustee shall collect the income of the trust property and may in his discretion, apply the net income to the payment of premiums on any life insurance policy owned by the trust. If the net income is insufficient to pay such premiums, the Trustee may notify in writing the Settlors and the beneficiaries of the trust of such insufficiency and give them the opportunity to furnish the necessary funds. If neither the Settlors nor any of the beneficiaries furnish the funds necessary to pay the premiums, the Trustee may, but is not required to obtain the funds required to pay such premiums by selling a portion of the trust principal, or borrowing on the security of the trust principal, by borrowing against the cash surrender value of the policy to pay premiums on other policies. The Trustee is also authorized to convert such policy to paid up or extended term insurance if the Trust Fund does not have the necessary funds to pay the premiums. If no funds are available for the payment of premiums on the policy, the Trustee is authorized to distribute such policy to the beneficiaries of the Trust named hereunder living at the time of the distribution.

(b)   If there is any trust income remaining after the payment of premiums in accordance with (a) above, such income shall be added to the principal of the Trust.

(c)   During the lifetime of either of the Settlors, any direct, indirect or deemed transfer to the Trust, whether in cash or other property, shall be subject to withdrawal pro rata under the provisions of this article by the beneficiaries of this Trust (herein this paragraph and in paragraph (d) following referred to as the "Donees"). Each pro rated right of withdrawal shall not exceed an amount for each Donee of the greater of Twenty Thousand Dollars ($20,000) or the amount of the gift tax annual exclusion under Section 2503(b) and 2513 of the Internal Revenue Code of 1986, as amended from time to time. The Trustee shall notify the Donees, in writing, of its receipt of any property over which their power of withdrawal can be exercised. Within thirty (30) days after their receipt of such notice, the Donees may exercise their power of withdrawal by informing the Trustee, in writing, of the amount they are withdrawing. If the Donees do not exercise their power of withdrawal within such thirty (30) day period, their power shall lapse with respect to the property covered by the notification. The Trustee is directed to hold a sufficient amount of the trust property in cash or in a form readily convertible to cash so that it may satisfy any exercise by the donees of their power of withdrawal. The Trustee may satisfy the exercise of any withdrawal right by distributing to the donee cash or other property, including life insurance policies. If any of the Donees is a minor or is otherwise under a disability, such as incompetency, guardian, committee, conservator or other authorized representative of the Donees may exercise the power of withdrawal on that Donee's behalf provided that under no circumstances may either of the Settlors so act on behalf of the Donees. If any Donee files for bankruptcy, that Donee's power of withdrawal shall be forfeited.

(d)   Notwithstanding any of the provisions above, if, upon the termination or lapse of any power of withdrawal, the Donee holding the power would be deemed to have made a taxable gift for federal gift tax purposes, such power shall continue in existence with respect to the amount that would have been a taxable gift, except to the extent it shall thereafter terminate as provided in this paragraph. Such power shall terminate as soon as and to the extent that termination shall not result in a taxable gift by the Donee holding the power.

5. Trustee's Duties Upon the Death of Either or Both Settlors. Upon the death of either or both of the Settlors, the Trustee shall receive such sums of money as shall be due it under the terms of the policies of life insurance, including double indemnity benefits, and hold them in trust for the uses set forth. To facilitate the receipt of these sums of money, the Trustee shall have the power to execute and deliver receipts and other instruments, to compromise or adjust disputed claims in the manner as is in it's sole discretion, to use any funds in its hands, whether principal or income, to pay the costs and expenses, including attorney's fees, of bringing an action for the collection of the proceeds of any policy, and may reimburse itself for any advances made for such purposes. Upon payment to the Trustee of the amounts due under the policies of insurance, the insurance companies issuing these policies shall be relieved of all further liability and no company shall be under any responsibility to see to the performance of the trust.

6. Dispositive Provisions.

(a)   Lifetime Trust. During the lifetime of the Settlors, the Trustee shall hold all of the Trust Estate for the benefit of the children of the Settlor, (hereinafter referred to collectively as the "Beneficiaries" or individually as a "Beneficiary"). The Trustee shall, so long as at least one of the

Settlors is alive, maintain the principal and accumulate all income within the Trust.

(b) *Death of Both of the Settlors.* Upon the death of both of the Settlors, the Trustees shall divide the Trust Estate, as then constituted, into equal shares per stirpes so that there will be one share for each of the Beneficiaries named above. The income and principal of each of such shares shall be held and disposed of as hereinafter provided:

    (i)   The income from each share so provided for each Beneficiary shall be paid in convenient installments to such Beneficiary. In addition to income, the Trustee shall be fully authorized to pay or expend and apply for the benefit of such Beneficiary such sums from the principal of his or her share as the Trustee considers necessary or desirable from time to time for his or her medical care, maintenance, education (including college education, both graduate and undergraduate), and support, taking into consideration all other income available to such beneficiary for such purposes from all sources known to the Trustee.

    (ii)   When a Beneficiary reaches the age of forty (40) years, or upon division of the Trust into shares if such Beneficiary has then reached such age, the Trustee shall distribute to such Beneficiary one-third (1/3) in value of the principal of his or her share, then held hereunder; when a Beneficiary reaches the age of forty-five (45) years, or upon division of the Trust into shares if such child has then reached such age, the Trustee shall distribute to such Beneficiary one-half (1/2) in value of the principal of his or her share, then held hereunder; and when a Beneficiary reaches the age of fifty (50) years, or upon division of the Trust into shares, if such child has then reached such age, the Trustee shall distribute to such Beneficiary the balance of his or her share.

    (iii)   In the event of the death of a Beneficiary prior to complete distribution of his or her share, or at the time such share is created, if such Beneficiary is then dead, then upon such Beneficiary's death or upon the setting up of such Beneficiary's share or the remainder thereof, the aforesaid shall be distributed per stirpes to his or her then living issue, if any, or if none then per stirpes to the then living issue of the Settlors, the share of any Beneficiary whose original share is then being held in trust to be added to and treated as part of that trust. If no child of the Settlors, nor the issue of any deceased child of the Settlors is living, then the proceeds of the Trust Estate shall be distributed to the heirs at law of

7. Income Accumulation. The Trustees shall accumulate income in whole or in part, if in it's discretion such income is not required for the purposes of this Trust in a particular year. Accumulated income shall be added to principal and may be expended in the same manner as principal.

8. Irrevocability. The Settlors hereby declare that this Trust Agreement is irrevocable, and cannot be altered, amended, or revoked at any time.

9. Powers of Trustee. The proceeds of the insurance policies, together with all other property held or which may be acquired by the Trustee hereunder, shall constitute the Trust Estate. In addition to the powers conferred by the common law, by statute, or by other provisions hereof, the Trustee is hereby empowered:

    (a)   to hold, possess, manage and control the Trust Estate for the purposes herein set forth;

    (b)   to invest and reinvest all or any part of the Trust Estate in such stocks, bonds, mutual funds, common trust funds, securities or other property, real or personal, including stock or other securities of any corporate fiduciary or of a holding company controlling said fiduciary, as in the Trustee's discretion Trustee shall deem proper, without regard to statutes limiting the property which Trustee may purchase;

    (c)   to sell, transfer, exchange, or otherwise dispose of, any part of the Trust Estate, for cash or on terms, at public or private sale, and to pledge or encumber the same;

    (d)   to lease any real estate held hereunder for any term, notwithstanding the duration of the Trust;

    (e)   to execute and deliver any deeds, leases, assignment or other instruments as may be necessary to carry out the provisions of this Trust;

    (f)   to open and maintain in the name of the Trust, bank accounts, safe deposit boxes and other adequate measures for the safeguarding of property;

(g) to exercise any subscription right in connection with any security held hereunder, and to consent to or participate in any reorganization, consolidation, or merger of any corporation;

(h) to make any distribution hereunder either in kind or in money. Distributions in kind shall be made at the market value of the property distributed and the Trustee may, in Trustee's discretion, cause the share to be transferred to any distributee to be composed of property like or different from that transferred to any other distributee;

(i) to conduct any business which may become a part of the Trust Estate for such period as the Trustees may deem proper, with power to borrow money and pledge the assets of such business, and to delegate such powers to any partner, manager or employee, without liability for any loss occurring therein. The Trustee may make public or private sale of such business, and the real and personal property thereof, at such time or times, and for such price or prices, and upon such terms as to cash and credit, with or without security for the purchase price, as the Trustee may deem best;

(j) The Trustee may, if the Trustee deems it wise, and without being required to obtain leave of court, organize a corporation to carry on such business, if unincorporated, by itself or jointly with others, and may contribute all or part of the property of such business as capital to such corporation and may accept stock in the corporation in lieu thereof. Similarly, the Trustee may dissolve any corporation carrying on any such business and may operate such business in any other form that the Trustee in Trustee's discretion, deems appropriate;

(k) to engage attorneys, accountants, agents, custodians, clerks, investment counsel and such other persons as the Trustee may deem advisable, and to make such payments therefore as the Trustee may deem reasonable, and to charge the expenses thereof to income or principal as the Trustee may determine, and to delegate to such persons any discretion which the Trustee may deem proper;

(l) to do all such acts, take all such proceedings and to exercise all rights and privileges, although not hereinbefore specifically mentioned, with relation to any such property, as if the absolute owners thereof, and in connection therewith to make, execute and deliver any instruments and to enter into any covenants or agreements binding any trust created hereunder;

(m)   to purchase securities on margins and to rehypothecate same.

10. Compensation of Trustees. The Trustee shall be reimbursed out of the trust estate for any advances made by him and for all reasonable expenses incurred in the management and protection of the trust estate, and for the employment of any agents, attorneys, accountants, and investment analysts and the like engaged by it for the protection and administration of the trust estate.

11. Bond and Liability of Trustee. Neither the original Trustee nor any successor Trustee shall be required to give any bond or security for the faithful performance of their duties. However, if any bond is required by law, then the bond shall be in such minimum amount as to satisfy the requirements of the law. Any Trustee shall be liable only for his own willful breach of trust and for fraud and not for any honest error in judgment. In any agreement or contract made by the Trustees on behalf of the trust estate, such Trustee shall be authorized to stipulate and provide against personal liability on such contracts, and the rights and obligations created by virtue of such contract or contracts shall belong to the trust estate.

12. Spendthrift Provision. The beneficiaries shall have no right to anticipate, to pledge, to encumber or hypothecate or in any other manner to alienate his interest in either the income or the principal of the trust estate and his interest shall not be liable for his debts, contracts, or engagements or subject to execution, attachment, sequestration, or other legal process other than as specifically provided in accordance with these terms.

13. Trustee's Account. The Trustee shall keep a complete and permanent record of all receipts and investments and disbursements made for or on behalf of or on account of the trust estate. The Trustee shall render an account annually and shall make available for inspection the annual account to those beneficiaries who are entitled to apply for benefits in accordance with the terms of this Trust Agreement. Whenever requested to do so by any of the beneficiaries, the books of the Trustee shall be open to the inspection of the beneficiary at all reasonable times. Additionally, if this trust is funded during the life of the Settlors, then an annual account shall be sent to the Settlors by the Trustee.

14. Succession and Resignation of Trustee. The Trustee named in this Deed of Trust may resign without accounting or Court approval at any time by a written notice of resignation delivered to Settlors, if living, or if not, then to the successor Trustee which notice shall thereupon be attached to this Agreement. In the event of such resignation, a successor Trustee may be appointed by the Settlors during their lifetime, or, after both of their deaths, by any court having jurisdiction over the Trust. Any successor Trustee thus appointed shall succeed to all the duties and to all the powers, including discretionary powers, granted to the original Trustee.

15. Termination of Trust. Notwithstanding anything herein to the contrary, unless sooner terminated under other provisions hereto, all trusts herein created shall terminate twenty-one (21) years after the death of the last survivor of the Settlors, their children and grandchildren living at such time as this instrument becomes irrevocable and, upon such termination, the then Trustee shall distribute the remaining principal and income in the trust so terminated to the person or persons then entitled to receive the income therefrom in the proportions in which they are so entitled.

16. Separability. If any provisions of this Trust Agreement shall be held invalid or unenforceable, the remaining provisions shall continue to be fully effective.

17. Law Governing Trusts. All questions pertaining to the administration of this Trust or the construction or validity of this Trust shall be governed by the law of the State of

18. Gender and Number. Words importing the singular number and masculine gender herein, shall be understood to apply to one or more persons and to females as well as males.

IN WITNESS WHEREOF, the Settlors and the Trustee have set their hands and have caused this Trust Agreement to be executed on the day and year first above written.

WITNESS:

_____

Settlor:

_____

Settlor:

_____

Trustee:

_____

Partnerships and Corporations

8

There are essentially three ways in which a business can be conducted:

- The sole proprietorship in which an individual operates a business under his or her own name and assumes all of the liability for the debts of the business.

- The partnership in which two or more persons form an association to carry on a business for profit as co-owners. Although the partnership entity is liable for the debts of the business, the partners themselves are jointly liable for all debts and liabilities. Partners, in a very real sense, bear the same potential liabilities as a sole proprietor. There is, however, a second form of partnership, known as the limited partnership, which has two categories of partners. One of those categories consists of limited partners whose liability for the debts of the business is restricted solely to the amount they invested to purchase their limited partnership interest. This form of limited partnership, as we shall see, can provide an invaluable tool in an asset protection program.

- The corporation is an invaluable asset protection tool. It shields all of its participants from liability for the debts of

the business. Properly structured, a corporation can provide the maximum protection against liability to third persons while offering the most attractive tax benefits to the owners of the business.

Before analyzing each of these business forms, it is important that you recognize the various factors involved in choosing one of these tools. So, for example, the first questions you must ask yourself are:

(1) Am I looking for a business form primarily to protect me against the claims arising out of the operations of my business or profession? If so, then you'll probably want to consider the corporation as your primary tool.

(2) Am I looking for a business form as an asset protection tool? The assumption here is that the business form will not actively operate a trade or profession, but will be used as a "safety deposit box" into which assets can be poured in order to protect them from attack.

(3) Will the business form create profits subject to federal or state taxation? If so, then you will find that certain forms are more favorable than others.

With these considerations in mind, let's take a look at the three categories of business forms.

General Partnerships and Sole Proprietorships

Neither the general partnership nor the sole proprietorship can serve a meaningful role in an asset protection program. In fact, each is the very antithesis of an asset protection tool. As noted above, the sole proprietor and the partner in a general partnership can be held liable for all of the debts of the business if the enterprise is unable to meet its obligations. This means that the personal—non-business—assets of the sole proprietor or partner can be attacked to satisfy the debts of the business. This potential liability exceeds ordinary business debts; it even includes liability imposed upon the business because of an employee's negligence. Assume, for example, that you operate a retail food shop and an employee carelessly stacks a soft drink display. The display topples over, severely injuring a passing shopper. That shopper's ten million dollar lawsuit will name the business, its proprietor or partners, and the stock clerk as the defendants in the lawsuit. If your business (and the insurance it carries) is not enough to satisfy the claim, then the plaintiff will come after your personal assets.

The sole proprietorship and the general partnership do provide several "alleged" benefits as business forms. Unlike corporations or limited partnerships, sole proprietorships can be formed without special filings in the state in which they operate. However, the filings for a limited partnership or corporation are rather simple, straightforward, and relatively inexpensive. As we'll explain a bit later in this chapter, you can form your own corporation simply and inexpensively.

The other key advantage to the sole proprietorship is that it permits the business owner to avoid the double taxation that can be imposed on a corporation's profits. Again, this advantage is illusory since (1) a corporation can be formed so that it enjoys partnership-like tax treatment, and (2) a limited partnership, by definition, enjoys the single tax treatment of partnerships.

It is clear, therefore, that neither the sole proprietorship nor the general partnership offers any advantages to be had for the individual who is concerned with shielding assets. Not only do these two business modes fail to protect any assets that may be placed in their care, but they can generate added exposure with respect to business obligations they create.

Understanding the Limited Partnership

A limited partnership is a business form that utilizes the best features of the corporation and the partnership. It receives the same favorable tax treatment that partnerships are accorded, and it provides the benefits of limited liability for its passive investors. The limited partnership is a business that consists of at least one general partner who manages the business and at least one limited partner, who as a passive investor, has no active voice in the management of the business and who cannot be held liable for the business's debts.

The general partner in a limited partnership is much like the partner in an ordinary partnership. The general partner can be held personally liable for the debts of the business. But, the general partner need not be a natural person, i.e., a human being. A corporation can be a general partner, and it will be liable for the debts of the limited partnership to the extent that it has assets.

The limited partners more closely resemble shareholders in a corporation than they do partners in a general partnership. A limited partner has no liability to third persons who have claims against the business. In fact, the total exposure of the limited partner is the investment he or she may have made in the business.

Because it offers the benefit of limited liability for its limited partners, a limited partnership can be created only if a state statute authorizes its existence. Except for Louisiana, every state authorizes the creation of limited partnerships. Most states have adopted a law based on the Uniform Limited Partnership Act; the few that have not adopted that act follow the revised Uniform Limited Partnership Act. Essentially, the two laws are quite similar. This means that there is one basic approach in the United States to the rules governing limited partnerships.

For our purposes, the limited partnership has the following attributes:

(1)   It must file a limited partnership certificate with the state in which it is to be created. The certificate itself is fairly straightforward (a model form is included at the end of this chapter), and the filing fees are inexpensive.

(2)   There must be at least one general and one limited partner.

(3)   The limited partnership need not have a limited life span. The death, retirement, or insanity of a limited partner does not end the existence of a limited partnership. Nor does the assignment of a limited partner's interest end the business's life span. The death, retirement, or insanity of a general partner, however, can end the business's life, unless the certificate filed with the state provides that the business will be continued with new general partners.

(4)   Although most people associate the limited partnership with real estate syndications, there is no limit on the types of business in which a limited partnership can engage.

(5)   General partners are held liable for the debts of the business to the same extent that they would be held liable to third persons if they were partners in an ordinary partnership. They are viewed as fiduciaries of the limited partners, which means that they must manage the business in accordance with the highest standards of good faith.

(6)   Limited partners have virtually no role in the management of the business and are not liable to outsiders for the debts of the business.

Although the law does not set a limit on the number of general partners a limited partnership can have, we will assume that the business will have only one general partner. That person's rights, duties and, most importantly, liabilities are identical to those of the partner in an ordinary partnership. The general partner makes all of the business decisions and sees to it that they are carried out. He or she bears all of the responsibility for the debts of the business if there are not sufficient assets to meet the claims of creditors.

Given the general partner's liability for the business's debts, how does a limited

The General Partner's Role

partnership fit in your asset protection program? This hurdle is easily overcome. First, the general partner can be a corporation formed primarily for this purpose. There is no requirement that the corporation have a specific amount of assets. In fact, most states permit a corporation to be formed with only minimal capitalization. Second, if the purpose of the limited partnership is solely to manage the assets put into it, then there is no need to fear the claims of third persons against the business. The business under those circumstances will have little, if any, basis on which to create debts to trade creditors or accidentally injure others.

Now, let us assume that you have put all of your assets into a limited partnership and that you are the general partner. You take back a one percent interest in the company and make family members the limited partners. Your personal creditors now can only go against your one percent interest in the limited partnership. But, they can only get the income which that one percent interest provides; they cannot take your place as the general partner of the business. At the same time, however, you obtain the following benefits:

(1) You maintain control over the manner in which those assets will be managed.

(2) You maintain control over the way in which the income of the limited partnership will be distributed, e.g., you can arrange to have the limited partnership pay yourself an appropriate salary for your services as a general partner.

(3) In the event of your death, the assets themselves will remain with the limited partners you have chosen, and a properly drafted limited partnership agreement will permit the limited partners to select a new general partner. Essentially, the bulk of your assets will not have to go through probate (the one percent holding that you retained may have to go through probate).

(4) You've adopted a business form that restricts the federal and state taxing authorities to only one bite out of your income.

The Role of the Limited Partner

As we've noted above, the role of the limited partner is very restricted. In return for that limited participation, the limited partner enjoys complete protection against liability for the debts of the business. In fact, the only risk the limited partner runs is that he or she will lose the investment he or she may have made in the business.

As we noted above in our discussion of general partners, the limited partnership that is created as an asset protection tool is likely to have as its sole purpose the protection of the assets put into the business. The limited partnership, therefore, is not likely to engage in efforts that will create liability for trade debts or physical injuries to others. But, what of the claims of creditors or others against a limited partner for debts that were incurred outside of the limited partnership? Essentially, the uniform acts governing this form of business put those creditors behind a rather large eight ball.

Let's start with a look at the Uniform Limited Partnership Act and see how it words its governing provision. Section 22 of that Act provides:

"(1) On due application to a court of competent jurisdiction by any judgment creditor of a limited partner, the court may charge the interest of the indebted limited partner with payment of the unsatisfied amount of the judgment debt; and may appoint a receiver, and make all other orders, directions, and inquiries which the circumstances of the case may require.

"(2) The interest may be redeemed with the separate property of any general partner, but may not be redeemed with partnership property.

"(3) The remedies conferred by paragraph (1) shall not be deemed exclusive of others which may exist.

"(4) Nothing in this act shall be held to deprive a limited partner of his statutory exemption."

The plain English meaning of the statute is that a creditor must overcome a series of hurdles, and even then can only obtain a very limited benefit from a successful challenge. These are the obstacles the creditor must overcome:

(1) It must obtain a judgment against the limited partner, i.e., hire counsel, go to court, try the case and succeed. (In some states, the creditor need not wait until the suit is concluded before attaching the debtor's assets, but even in those states, the following obstacles remain in place.)

(2) Have a court issue a charging order against the limited partner's interest. The charging order, however, does not give the creditor title to the limited partner's interest in the business. Instead it merely gives the creditor the right to receive the debtor's income from the limited partnership, and, if the limited partnership eventually dissolves, the debtor's share of the partnership's assets. However, there is no guaranty that the general partner will distribute profits to the limited partners or that the business will be dissolved during the creditor's lifetime.

(3) The creditor can foreclose on the limited partner's interest and call for a foreclosure sale of that interest. Common sense dictates that such a forced sale will bring little if anything for the debtor's interest. How much will be bid if the potential buyer has every reason to believe the general partner will not make payments of profits? Further, the potential buyer does not get a right to receive an accounting on the business operations or to participate as a limited partner. All such a buyer would receive is the right to receive any payments that will be made to the debtor.

As a practical matter, such a creditor will probably have to agree to a rather insignificant cash settlement under which the remaining limited partners acquire the debtor's interest in the business.

Example:

To recognize the significance of the obstacles facing a creditor, consider the following scenario. In order to protect his assets, Mr. Smith creates a limited partnership into which he places all of his assets. He names his wife and three children as limited partners, and they each invest a minimal amount in the limited partnership. Mr. Smith is the general partner and retains a one percent interest in the business. Mr. Smith, except for his one percent interest in the partnership, has no assets. He knows that he will have income (salary) from the business and that he will completely control the assets he has put into the business.

Now assume that three years pass, and a bank has foreclosed on a $25,000 loan made to one of Mr. Smith's children. The bank obtains a judgment and finds out that the child has only one asset, a twenty-five percent interest in the limited partnership. It obtains a charging order and demands that the limited partnership make payments to it of income due the child. Mr. Smith cheerfully agrees, but points out that the partnership has not made any payments for the past two years and is unlikely to make any for the next ten years.

If the other limited partners now offer to buy the bank's interest in the debtor's right to profits (remember, the bank cannot replace the debtor as a limited partner) for perhaps ten to twenty cents on the dollar, is the bank in a position to refuse? It doesn't have an interest it can successfully dispose of at a forced sale. It can't replace the general partner who obviously will not make payments to the limited partners. It either takes what it can get now or it will be forced to sit on a useless interest.

Protecting Your Status as a Limited Partner

Since one of the major advantages of the limited partnership is its ability to immunize its passive investors from liability, it is vital that you do nothing to jeopardize that status. A limited partner can be treated as a general partner if he or she goes beyond the statutory or judicial limits on their rights. As a limited partner, you cannot take part in the management of the enterprise. Under the Uniform Acts and court decisions interpreting those acts, you are entitled to do the following:

- Act as an independent contractor for the business.

- Agree to work as an employee or agent of the limited partnership or the general partner.

- Consult with and give non-binding advice to the general partner. You should, however, do this sparingly and ensure that there is something in writing that demonstrates you were supplying non-binding advice as opposed to a direct order.

- Guarantee debts of the business (although this would seem to be a self-defeating gesture in an asset protection program).

- Approve or disapprove an amendment to the partnership agreement.

- Vote on the following matters: (1) the dissolution and wind up of the business; (2) the sale, exchange, lease, mortgage, pledge or other transfer of all or substantially all of the assets of the business if the transaction does not occur in the ordinary course of business (A real estate limited partnership which is in business to sell real property may, for example, regularly sell all of its holdings in the regular course of its business. A retail shop, however, would not sell all of its inventory and the lease on its shop in the ordinary course of its business which is to sell goods at retail); (3) incurring debt other than in the ordinary course of the partnership's business; (4) changing the nature of the business; or (5) removing a general partner.

One other precaution: if a limited partner allows his or her name to be used in the title of the business, then that person will be treated as if he or she is a general partner.

Protecting the Limited Partnership's Tax Status

A key advantage of the limited partnership is that its profits are taxed only once—when they are received by the limited partners. The corporate form usually sees its profits taxed twice—once as profits earned by the corporation, and again in the hands of its shareholders when they receive the remainder of those after-tax profits as dividends. In one circumstance, the single taxation benefit can be lost, and the limited partnership treated as a corporation for tax purposes. This happens if a corporation is used as the only general partner and it does not have enough assets to satisfy the limited partnership's debts. If, however, your limited partnership is adopted solely to hold and manage assets, it is highly unlikely that the business will ever be in a position where it will have sufficient debts to create a prob-

lem. In such cases it is not even necessary to use a corporation as the general partner.

The use of a corporation as a general partner is usually restricted to situations where the business actively conducts activities that will create elements of risk, e.g., a real estate construction venture. In such cases, the corporation that serves as a general partner must have at least $250,000 or 15 percent of the full amount of the limited partners' contributions; if the contributions total over $2.5 million, the corporate general partner must have a net worth of no less than 10 percent of the limited partner's contributions. These requirements, however, suggest that in most situations where an active business is to be run by individuals concerned with federal income tax demands, an S corporation is the entity of choice.

Role of the Corporation in an Asset Protection Program

Although the corporation plays a vital role in any asset protection program, its role should not be viewed as one that offers complete protection in all circumstances. At most, a corporation can protect you from liability arising out of the conduct of a business. Unlike the limited partnership, it will not shield your personal assets from an attack by third persons based on non-corporate debts you may have.

Corporations are entities that were created by legislatures in order to make it possible for entrepreneurs to raise money from a broad group of investors. In order to convince people to invest in enterprises that required vast amounts of capital, the legislatures introduced the concept of limited liability, i.e., the business entity—not those who operated or invested in it—would be liable for its debts. Although it is an artificial entity, a corporation is viewed as a person by the law. As an entity, it bears the responsibility for its debts. In the absence of fraud on their part, the corporation's shareholders, directors and officers are not liable for the debts of the business.

The structure of the corporation is quite simple. Its owners are its shareholders, the people who invest the money with which the corporation was created and funded. The directors are the "brain" of the corporation. Elected by shareholders, the directors establish the company's policies and appoint officers to carry out those policies.

The position taken by the legislatures that created the laws under which corporations are formed is that when people deal with a corporation, they are dealing with that entity and not its shareholders, directors or officers. It is for that reason that only the corporation and not its directors, officers or shareholders is held liable for the debts of the business.

Since the corporation is liable for money it borrows and injuries it may cause, it is clearly the best form of doing business for an operating company. Whatever liability it incurs simply does not pass through to its directors, officers or shareholders. But, every plus usually has its minus, and that is true of the corporation. Although we'll explain how you can surmount them, here are the negatives you must be prepared to cope with:

Problem #1:

A corporation cannot protect you from liability for injuries you may cause. A doctor who incorporates and proceeds to negligently perform an operation can be held personally liable for his negligence along with his corporation. If you operate a company car and negligently injure someone, both you and the corporation that employs you can be held liable for the injury. Where the corporation protects you is when the injury is caused by a different employee. In that case, unless you contributed to the injury, only the employee and the corporation can be held liable to an injured third person.

Response:

For the most part, if you are active in an operating business, you should take care to purchase sufficient insurance to cover potential liability for your own acts. The policy can be carried by the corporation, just so long as it protects you. Even if you have adopted various of the approaches contained in this book to make yourself judgment proof, sound financial planning virtually demands that you insure against third party claims based on your alleged negligent performance of your trade, business or profession.

Problem #2:

Since your corporation is liable for its debts, your investment in it is at risk to those with claims against the business. Assume, for example, that you own all of the shares of a corporation that operates a dry cleaning establishment. The corporation owns all of the equipment in the store and the real estate on which it stands. Assume those assets are worth $500,000. Assume also that your business is adequately insured, and that a claim is brought against it that exceeds the amount of the insurance. Although you personally may not be liable on the claim, the corporation's assets—valued at one-half of a million dollars—can be used to satisfy the claim.

Response:

You can form two corporations: one to operate the business and a second to own the assets used by the first corporation. So, for example, you can form a corporation that acquires both the real estate and the equipment needed to operate a dry cleaning store and lease both the equipment and the real estate to a corporation that operates the business. If the operating corporation is sued by an injured party, its insurance will be used to cover the problem. If the insurance is inadequate, the corporation that acts as the lessor of the equipment and the real estate is not liable to an injured third party since it had nothing to do with the injury. Similarly, trade creditors of the operating corporation do not have a claim against the lessor for the debts of the lessee.

Problem #3:

If you are a shareholder in your corporation (or any corporation), the shares you hold can be taken by your judgment creditors for non-business debts. Assume you are a doctor and you own a corporation that operates a franchised fast-food outlet. Your franchise has a fair market value of $300,000. Assume a patient sues you for malpractice and recovers an amount in excess of your malpractice insurance coverage. Your judgment creditor now takes your franchise by foreclosing on your shares of stock.

Response:

If you wish to be secure from such attacks, you have no choice but to consider placing your shares of stock in an irrevocable trust or a limited partnership. Either of those options will protect your investment, but both mean that you must sacrifice direct ownership. The limited partnership does offer you the benefit of continued income from your assets if you name yourself as the general partner of the limited partnership.

Problem #4:

Many corporations are C Corporations under the Internal Revenue Code. This means they are subject to double taxation, i.e., the profits earned by the corporation are subject to a corporate income tax, and the monies that remain after those taxes are subject to tax again when they are received as income (dividends) by shareholders. If your C Corporation is successful, the combined taxes can eat up approximately 60 percent of its profits. A partnership, by way of comparison, is not taxed; its profits flow through to its partners who are taxed at their own individual rates (28 percent maximum).

Response:

Consider the approach suggested in the response to Problem #2 above, except that you have the leasing corporation formed as an S Corporation and the operating corporation formed as a C Corporation. If the lease arrangements between the two corporations are structured properly, it is likely that the operating corporation will have very minimal profits on which taxes can be imposed. The bulk of the profits will be earned by the S Corporation which leases the real estate and equipment to the operating corporation. Why form an S Corporation? Because for most tax purposes it is treated as if it is a partnership, but in all other respects, i.e., liability, it is treated no differently than a C Corporation. In short, an S Corporation combines the best features of the partnership and the C Corporation.

The one drawback to an S Corporation is that it cannot provide medical or life insurance benefits and deduct the premiums as business expenses (neither can a partnership). A C Corporation, however, can deduct the costs of insurance premiums as business expenses. If your operating corporation is formed as a C Corporation, it can provide those benefits and deduct the cost of providing them from its income for tax purposes.

Problem #5:

Corporations cannot exist without the authorization of the state in which they are created. This means that a certificate of incorporation must be filed. If you intend to use both a C and an S Corporation, you'll have to make two filings. Isn't this an expensive, time consuming process?

Response:

Forming a corporation is easy, inexpensive, and can be accomplished in one day. After over a century of existence, legislatures have learned how to make the corporation accessible to business people.

Tip #1:

For a complete, easy-to-use guide to incorporation, see HOW TO

FORM YOUR OWN CORPORATION WITHOUT A LAWYER FOR UNDER $50, published by Enterprise Publishing, Inc., 725 North Market Street, Wilmington, DE 19801.

Tip #2:

For a step-by-step guide showing you how to form an S Corporation, see THE "S" CORPORATION HANDBOOK, published by Enterprise Publishing, Inc., 725 North Market Street, Wilmington, DE 19801.

Minimizing Risks Involved in Operating a Corporation

Although the corporation was expressly created by state legislatures to protect investors and operators of corporations from personal liability, there are certain precautions you must take to ensure that you do not lose that protection:

● Avoid making a personal guaranty on a corporate obligation. If you volunteer yourself as a co-signer or guarantor, then you are assuming the risk that you *personally* will have to repay the obligation.

● Always sign a contract, lease, loan document or other business paper in your corporate capacity. So, for example, always sign as "John Smith, President, ABC Corp." Never sign just as "John Smith." If you do not indicate you are signing for the corporation, a creditor may very well be able to show that you agreed to be liable under the agreement.

● Avoid, to the extent humanly possible, careless conduct that may create potential injury to third persons. This includes matters such as hiring qualified personnel to carry out business operations. So, for example, if you hire someone to drive a delivery van, make

sure that person is qualified to drive the vehicle. Don't just ask if he or she has a license; demand to see it before you hire the person. If you do not, and the person is unlicensed, you can be held liable for any injuries he or she may cause because you negligently allowed an unqualified person to perform a duty for you.

● Always make sure your corporation pays its taxes, be they withholding, Social Security, sales or any other form of tax. If it does not, you as an officer or controlling shareholder can be held personally liable to either the federal government or to the state government for unpaid taxes.

● Do not authorize your corporation to pay dividends unless there are profits to support the dividend payment. If dividends are paid when the corporation is losing money, its creditors can come after the individual directors of the corporation to recover monies improperly paid out as dividends.

● If your corporation's operations have any aspect that may have environmental impacts, seek out expert advice to determine whether those impacts violate state or federal law. If they do, correct them immediately. Under both federal and state law, if a cleanup is required and the corporation cannot foot the bill, directors, officers and even shareholders can be required to bear the cost of the cleanup.

Questions and Answers on Asset Protection

9

Q. May an IRS levy continue to take my paychecks as I earn them?

A. Yes. Section 6334 of the Internal Revenue Code authorizes a levy to be continuous until the time period has expired or the tax liability is satisfied.

Q. Can the IRS take my entire paycheck?

A. No. Section 6334(d) provides the statutory exemption to which you are entitled. The 1988 Tax Act changed the previous exemption amount and substituted the following formula:

The term "exempt amount" means an amount equal to the sum of—

   (i)   the standard deduction, and

   (ii) the aggregate amount of the deductions for personal exemptions allowed the taxpayer under section 151 in the taxable year in which such levy occurs, divided by 52.

Q. Which of my personal assets are exempt from IRS seizure?

A. Section 6334(a) lists the personal property that is exempt from IRS seizure. It includes:

1. "Such items of wearing apparel and such school books as are necessary for the taxpayer or for members of his family."

2. "If the taxpayer is the head of a family, so much of the fuel, provisions, furniture, and personal effects in his household, and of the arms for personal use, livestock, and poultry of the taxpayer, as does not exceed $1,650 in value."

3. "So many of the books and tools necessary for the trade, business, or profession of the taxpayer as do not exceed in the aggregate $1,100 in value."

Also exempt are such property as certain pension payments to railroad workers, workmen's compensation payments, and support payments to minors.

Q. How long does the IRS have to collect delinquent taxes?

A. The 1990 Tax Act extended the time the IRS has to collect an assessed tax from six to ten years. After the expiration of ten years, the IRS may not proceed against your property unless you have agreed to extend the time for collection. The form granting the extension is Form 900, Tax Collection Waiver. You may find the collection agent most uncooperative should you not consent to the extension. In fact, the agent may even seize all of the taxpayer's assets, without regard to the difficulties it places upon the taxpayer and his or her family.

Q. Can the IRS take my pension or retirement account?

A. Yes. All retirement monies, both qualified and nonqualified, are subject to attachment by the IRS. The Employee Retirement Income Security Act generally prohibits creditors from obtaining pension monies. The IRS is notably absent from that prohibition.

Q. How does the IRS know what you own?

A. You tell them, either voluntarily or indirectly. At collections, the collection agent will ask you to fill out Form 433 (see Chapter 4), particularly if you are asking for an offer and compromise of your liability. The IRS also has your previously filed income tax returns listing your securities holdings, interest bearing accounts, and showing whether you take a mortgage deduction for land that you own. Older returns will also show if you had any consumer loans that may be secured by an automobile or boat. Finally, the IRS has the authority to subpoena your records from your bank, stock broker, accountant, and any one else they may believe has records of your financial condition.

Q. Does a tax lien stop you from transferring real estate?

A. No. In general, the tax lien flows with the real estate. Therefore, the government is protected as long as the lien was "perfected". As a practical matter, however, the buyer will probably insist that the lien be satisfied at closing.

Q. Is there any benefit in transferring real estate to your spouse?

A. With respect to a tax liability, your spouse may be an innocent spouse. Property in your spouse's name, as long as it is not a fraudulent transfer, will be exempt from IRS liens.

Q. Should you and your spouse file separate tax returns?

A. From an asset protection standpoint, it is advantageous to file separately. A spouse who files separate tax returns is not responsible for the tax liability of the other spouse. However, separate filings may result in a larger tax bill. This is due to the fact that the tax law rates are higher for single individuals than they are for married couples.

Q. How does the homestead exemption effect the sale of real property?

A. In those states granting a homestead exemption, the property subject to the exemption may not be sold unless the purchase price exceeds the exemption amount. Therefore, states that provide unlimited homestead exemptions are desirable places for an individual to have a residence.

Q. Can you continue to own property after filing for bankruptcy?

A. If you file for a Wage Earners Plan, you continue to own and control your assets. However, if you file a Chapter 7 bankruptcy, all non-exempt property is turned over to a Trustee.

Q. What if you cannot make your Wage Earner Plan payments for a short period of time?

A. If your ability to make the required payments under the plan will continue for an extended period, the Court will likely convert your plan to a Chapter 7; however, if the nonpayment will be temporary, the plan can usually be modified.

Q. When must your unsecured creditors file claims under a Chapter 13?

A. Your unsecured creditors are required to file their proof of claims within 90 days after the first scheduled meeting of creditors. Should they fail to do so, your debt to them will be discharged without any payment and they will be

unable to make a claim later. Remember that only your debts to creditors who are disclosed are discharged, so do not be fooled into thinking that by not listing creditors you will cause their claim to go away.

Q. Are there ways to protect family property if you must file for bankruptcy under Chapter 7?

A. Yes, your property can be effectively retained through the use of family limited partnerships, corporations, and business trusts. All members of the family have some form of an ownership interest in the entity. This may have originally been accomplished when each family member contributed assets to the business. In the alternative, the parents may have initially owned one hundred percent of the entity and subsequently gifted ownership interests to their children. Ultimately the ownership interest of the parent would be reduced to zero, but he or she would still be the managing person, e.g., trustee, president or managing general partner. Since the parent has no ownership interest in the entity, there are no assets for the bankruptcy court to take; however, always beware not to have completed a transfer transaction within one year of bankruptcy or the trustee may void the transfers as fraudulent conveyances.

Similarly, an individual could gift away his property prior to the bankruptcy. The Internal Revenue Code entitles each individual to annually gift, without tax liability, $10,000 per recipient, $20,000 for married couples. Further, each individual has a lifetime credit, known as the unified credit, equivalent to $600,000 of value transferred for less than adequate consideration. Accordingly, an individual might gift up to $600,000 plus $10,000 per recipient without incurring any tax liability. Assume a husband and wife have two married children and four grandchildren; they could gift $1,360,000 without incurring any tax liability for the gift. The amount is reached when the husband and wife each use the full $600,000 of their unified credit equivalency plus the $10,000 they gave to each child, each child's spouse and each grandchild. Subject to the earlier discussion of fraudulent conveyance, these gifts would be exempt from a bankruptcy proceeding involving the gifting parents. It is not difficult to imagine that after a bankruptcy, or even during bankruptcy, that the property in question will be loaned to the parents for their benefit. BE CAREFUL, SUCH ARRANGEMENTS MAY BE SUBJECT TO SCRUTINY BY THE BANKRUPTCY TRUSTEE.

Q. Can your creditors seize your interest in an inheritance?

A. Usually, creditors can attach your inheritance, but not before it is distributed to you. Many wills contain spendthrift clauses so that your creditors cannot anticipate your inheritance and receive your share directly from the estate.

Q. What should you do if you anticipate a large inheritance and have substantial creditors currently?

A. You have two strategies to follow to keep your creditors from taking your expected inheritance.

1. You may disclaim the inheritance, or

2. File for bankruptcy before the inheritance.

When you disclaim an inheritance, you are treated as if you were not alive and your share goes to the next level of beneficiaries. If your children or your spouse are at the next level, a disclaimer will be an effective tool to shield assets from your creditors.

Bankruptcy will discharge your debts. If done more than six months before the receipt of an inheritance, the inheritance will not be part of the bankrupt estate and will be exempt from the claims of your creditors. Recently, an individual who was the sole beneficiary of a million dollar estate, declared Chapter 7 bankruptcy to discharge a bank debt of $500,000. The bank was not even pressing its claim, as it was aware of the prospective inheritance. Needless to say, the bank was less than thrilled.

Q. Should you transfer your property to a trust or limited partnership instead of to your spouse?

A. There is no easy answer here. Emotional, rather than asset protection, concerns may prevail. The risk of divorce may negate your asset protection program. Similarly, you do not know that your spouse will continue to be the one who is less subject to creditors' claims. Finally, creditors may be successful in overturning a transfer to your spouse as a fraudulent transfer.

Q. Can you use a mortgage to protect your real estate?

A. Yes, a creditor who holds a mortgage has the greatest security in the property. All others stand in line after the mortgagee. Consider granting mortgages to family members to whom you owe money. For a non-mortgage debtor to collect against your property, he will have to pay off the mortgage holders who are ahead of him.

    You may consider remortgaging your real estate to strip out your equity in the property. For example, a parcel of land worth $200,000 may have a mortgage against it of $160,000. You might record additional mortgages in favor of your family of an additional $30,000. Your equity in the land is $10,000. A creditor with a $5,000 claim against you would have to sell the property and net $190,000 before he would realize anything from the sale.

Q. How should you protect yourself from liability as a director of a corporation?

A. The primary protection available to the director of a corporation is director's

and officer's liability insurance. As with most casualty insurance, this is an efficient use of dollars for the protection and peace of mind that it provides. Many corporations will offer a director an indemnification agreement. These agreements are fine as additional protection, but without liability insurance, the indemnification protection may prove to be valueless. If the business becomes insolvent or goes bankrupt, its directors and officers may be the owners of a worthless indemnity.

Q. Can property owned by your spouse be subject to attachment by your creditors?

A. No. Universally, the courts have recognized the separateness of ownership between husband and wife. Your property is not at risk from your spouse's creditors, and vice versa. The exception to this separate recognition is if the debt is a joint debt of both spouses.

Q. Can you be obligated to provide your creditors with a listing of your property prior to your creditors obtaining a judgment?

A. No. However, if your creditor becomes aware that you are disposing of your assets, he may ask the court to enjoin any fraudulent transfers. Such prohibition is an extraordinary power of the court which is exercised in only the most special circumstances.

Q. Are gifts to family members easily voidable?

A. Gifts to family members are subject to challenge as fraudulent transfers. Love and affection do not constitute consideration for a transfer. If you are insolvent after the gift, the courts will treat the transfer as fraudulent on its face.

Q. What is a spendthrift trust?

A. Classically, a spendthrift trust prohibits a creditor from reaching inside the trust to satisfy claims against either the grantors or the beneficiaries. The clause does not limit a creditor's ability to attach property after it comes out of the Trust. It is only a bar to enforcement procedures while the property is in the Trust.

Q. How can you protect newly acquired assets from prior judgments?

A. The primary way to protect newly acquired assets is to have them actually titled in your spouse's or children's name. If the assets are for a business venture, then for all parties involved it would be best to incorporate the business with your spouse or children holding the shares of the corporation and you being employed as an officer. In this fashion, you control the day-to-day use of the assets, but they are not "legally" yours for your personal creditors to be able to attach.

Q. How should you title assets that will be used in a risky start-up venture?

A. Most attorneys recommend that operating assets be maintained outside of the corporation and leased to the new venture. Assuming your corporation satisfies the legal requirements for formation and operation so that creditors cannot breach the corporate veil, the leased assets will be beyond the reach of creditors should the corporation fail.

There may also be tax advantages to leasing assets to a corporation. You will be receiving income from the corporation that may be "tax free" as a result of the depreciation deduction to which you are entitled.

You may leverage additional tax benefits by placing the assets in a minor's trust. The income is payable to the trust for the benefit of your children and, if they are over 14 years of age, the lease income is taxable at your children's tax rate, which is likely to be lower than your tax rate.

Q. Should real estate be included in your operating corporation?

A. An operating corporation should never own real estate. Your operating corporation is likely to be exposed to significant claims from creditors. Real estate can be the greatest source of equity. Keep it outside the grasp of your creditors, by leasing the real estate to the corporation.

Q. Must a professional maintain malpractice insurance?

A. The answer depends on state law. Many states require professionals to have insurance. For example, it is an ethical violation for an attorney not to have insurance. The failure to purchase malpractice insurance can cause a lawyer to be suspended from the practice of law. In the past, many professionals chose to "go naked" to discourage claims. This is both foolish and foolhardy. Going naked may leave you truly out in the cold without your family home and/or other possessions. In today's litigious society, the rule should be to purchase as much insurance as possible.

Q. What is the best way to protect against risk?

A. Insurance is the most cost efficient and reasonable way to protect the bulk of your assets from a claim. You should have the following types of insurance:

1. *Automobile Insurance.* In many states the law requires you to have this insurance, but you may be surprised at how many people drive without protection because of the expense. Check with your insurance agent and purchase enough insurance to give you liability protection. In today's litigious times, you should maintain at least $100,000/$300,000 coverage, particularly if you have a home. It would be a tragedy compounded if you are in an accident, get sued and your insurance only covers $50,000, and a judgment is rendered for $200,000. The injured person will probably try to go after your home to collect his or her claim. It is this type of threat that your asset protection planning should seek to avoid.

2. *Homeowner's Insurance.* Homeowner's insurance protects you

from injury claims by people who are on your property. It is inexpensive, and many mortgage companies provide for it in your escrow account. One million dollars is the recommended coverage to provide for unforeseen situations.

3. *Umbrella Coverage.* This is the most underutilized form of insurance; yet it is the most economical of all liability insurance. It provides an additional layer of coverage on top of your current insurance. The charge is usually nominal for one million dollars of coverage. Also, ask your insurance agent if an umbrella policy will allow you to reduce your other coverage amounts—thereby saving additional money. Umbrella coverage also provides protection for items that may not be covered by your homeowner's insurance, i.e., libel and slander claims.

Index